P9-CDW-042

IN THE ZONE

HOW TO GET OVER YOUR OBSTACLES AND SUCCEED

MARK CREAR PhD

Abingdon Press™
Nashville

IN THE ZONE:
HOW TO GET OVER YOUR OBSTACLES AND SUCCEED

Copyright © 2013 by Mark Crear

All rights reserved.

No part of this work may be reproduced or transmitted in any form or by any means, electronic or mechanical, including photocopying and recording, or by any information storage or retrieval system, except as may be expressly permitted by the 1976 Copyright Act or in writing from the publisher. Requests for permission should be addressed to Permissions, The United Methodist Publishing House, P.O. Box 801, 201 Eighth Avenue South, Nashville, TN 37202-0801 or permissions@umpublishing.org.

Library of Congress Cataloging-in-Publication Data

Crear, Mark.
    In the zone : how to get over your obstacles and succeed / Mark Crear, PhD.
      pages cm
    ISBN 978-1-4267-7202-3 (adhesive binding, pbk./trade : alk. paper) 1. Success—Religious aspects—Christianity. I. Title.
    BV4598.3.C74 2014
    248.4—dc23

                                                                        2013042566

Unless otherwise noted, Scripture quotations are from the New Revised Standard Version of the Bible, copyright 1989, Division of Christian Education of the National Council of the Churches of Christ in the United States of America. Used by permission. All rights reserved.

Scripture quotations marked KJV are from The Authorized (King James) Version. Rights in the Authorized Version in the United Kingdom are vested in the Crown. Reproduced by permission of the Crown's patentee, Cambridge University Press.

Scripture quotations noted CEB are from the Common English Bible. Copyright © 2011 by the Common English Bible. All rights reserved. Used by permission. www.CommonEnglish-Bible.com.

13 14 15 16 17 18 19 20 21 22—10 9 8 7 6 5 4 3 2 1

MANUFACTURED IN THE UNITED STATES OF AMERICA

CONTENTS

CONTENTS

ACKNOWLEDGMENTS

For His abiding love and guidance throughout the "hurdles" in my life, I give all honor and glory to my Lord and Savior, Jesus Christ.

Like the famous saying goes, "teamwork makes the dream work" is indeed an accurate summery of this project. Many personal life lessons through ups and downs, victories and losses have shaped the character and content of my self and the content of this book. I acknowledge and personally thank all of those who shared their story with me as well as those who assisted me when I was faced with my life's hurdles.

Last but not lest, I offer special thanks to Avalyn "Fam's" Smith for her unwavering support and belief in me and in the ministry in which we were assigned.

INTRODUCTION

"Runners, take your mark. . . . Set. . . . Go!" This command has motivated me for most of my life. For me, it has always been about more than running a race for a medal; it's been about living a successful life. But as things turned out, the 110-meter high hurdles became a metaphor for my life. This event came to signify the hurdles that I had to overcome. Sometimes I cleared the hurdles smoothly, sometimes I hit them, and sometimes I tipped them over and fell. But regardless of the scenario, I got back up and finished the race. Perhaps you have a different metaphor for your life, but we're all trying for success, and we all encounter obstacles that get in the way.

Hurdles are an inevitable part of our lives. Whether you're a professional athlete, a student, the CEO of a big corporation, a pastor, a believer, or a nonbeliever, there is one sure guarantee: life is full of hurdles and obstacles to overcome. The key is how to overcome these hurdles and run to victory. But how is it that some people seem to overcome their hurdles faster than others? How is it that some people may even get over hurdles faster than you? Why do some bounce back after defeat and disaster easier than others? Why do some seem to always win and others to always lose? As a two-time Olympic medalist, I have learned a lot about obstacles—winning and losing—on and off the track. I have learned that more than anything else, the ability to overcome and deal with hurdles (expected and unexpected) is most important. People often ask me, "Mark, how did you do it? How did you run the Olympics and win a silver medal with a broken arm? How did you win the Olympic bronze medal with a double hernia?" I tell them, "It wasn't easy, but those are only two of the most obvious things I had to overcome. I'm just like you. When life throws up insurmountable hurdles, we can get back up, run, and win." Everybody has obstacles in life; they don't have to defeat you, but you do have to train and get ready to face them. You have to find the right practice routine and apply it diligently to your life. You need to be able to find the zone.

Like everyone, I've had trials and tribulations. And like too many others, my childhood was filled with emotional, physical, and mental abuse. I've had success and failure, but through it all I have discovered that there is a consistency in success that comes only from living in the zone. I have discovered a formula that works for me, a formula that might also help you to find, enter, and stay in your zone to overcome your hurdles and succeed.

We've all heard TV sports commentators talk about an athlete being "in the zone." Perhaps you've experienced it when you've pitched a game or given a difficult presentation. What's it like to be in the zone? It's as if you can't do anything wrong. All the pieces fall together effortlessly. Time might even seem to slow down for you. Everything is in sync. You can't miss. Nothing distracts you from your goal. You have heightened awareness. You feel at your peak and you perform at your best. But we also know that a lot of practice and effort go into *looking* effortless. An athlete who performs in the zone has spent countless hours practicing and thinking about all those pieces that *seem* to fit miraculously together in the heat of competition. And the ability to set distractions aside comes from a wealth of hard knocks. Being in the zone takes work and a disciplined approach to life. The goal of this book is to help you train for your race and overcome obstacles that will try to block your success.

COMPETING AND COMPETITION

In order to successfully hurdle over life's obstacles, you must learn how to compete. Once you discover how to compete, you will begin to become competitive—in a healthy sense. This is where many rise and fall. Igniting that competitiveness and competition spirit is what every coach, manager, and executive wants to do for their team. However, sometimes competition frightens individuals to the degree that they are unable to compete. The anxiety attached to competition causes some people to choke and go down in flames. The goal is to understand the nature of competition and how to embrace it, rather than simply react to it.

In order to compete, we must first understand where fear and self-doubt come from. Fear and self-doubt come from people's personal perceptions of themselves. The fact is that most people base their personal perceptions on social expectations. It reminds me of the time when I was standing in front of the mirror looking at myself, while asking my homeboys, "How do I look?" I remember one of my friends saying, "You tell me! You are the one looking in the mirror." It was at that moment I realized that in order to gain confidence in myself, I needed to establish my own set of criteria and standards. Otherwise, I would always be putting my faith, confidence, joy, and happiness in others' hands, and depending on other people's moods is not a fruitful way to determine my own response or how I think about myself.

Competing is the act of striving to gain or win something by defeating or establishing superiority over others who are trying to do the same. Competition is an inevitable part of life. Whenever you encounter another person, some competition and comparison occur. It's just the level of competition and comparison that is the question. I hear many people say that they aren't competitive or they don't want to compete. The fact is that we all compete. We compete for attention, love, recognition, and to get noticed. We may not compete to a significant degree all the time, but wherever and whenever we are passionate about something, we become competitive. Whenever one or more people are passionate about the same thing and striving to achieve the same goal, competition is born. You want something. If it's all that good, others will want it too. Competition can help us work harder, better, and more efficiently.

But competition can be unethical. I recall walking to the mall during the Christmas holiday. The parking lot was packed with cars and walkways were flooded with Christmas shoppers. My purpose of going to the mall was to get a pair of shoes for my son. Little did I know, it was Black Friday— the day after Thanksgiving when the Christmas buying season officially begins. In addition, Apple had just launched its latest iPhone, which was going on sale for half off. I couldn't believe my eyes! I saw individuals literally fighting and competing for parking spaces and long lines with people jostling to get as close to the front as possible. Judging by appearances, these folks wouldn't be caught dead competing on an athletic field.

Understand that everyone is competitive to a certain degree. The desire to be number one or get what we want is an individual measure that is usually based on the relevance of what is at stake, but some want to win at all costs. Unhealthy competition is cutthroat, meaning that a person is willing to be unethical and push others out of the way to get what he or she wants. Many of us lose focus and forget what the purpose of competition is. Competition is not intended to humiliate or destroy your opponent. Competition should provoke and produce respect and appreciation.

In 2001 at the IAAF Diamond League Track Meet, held in Zurich, Switzerland, there were two semifinal races, eight athletes in each race. In order to advance to the finals, you had to place in the top four in your heat. At this time, it was well known that I had a broken left arm. I broke my arm while training just two and a half weeks prior to this competition. It was quite swollen and so sore that the slightest touch sent excruciating pain throughout my entire body. Despite this, I chose not to have a cast put on it and instead ran bare-armed.

I was in lane four and one of my competitors from Germany, who was in lane three, decided to do something that was unsportsmanlike and, frankly, downright dirty! As the officials said, "Runners, take your mark," I noticed him intensely staring at my left arm. However, I paid no mind and prepared to race. *Bang!* As we rounded the first curve, I was in sixth place, trying to work my way up to be in the top four finishers. I gained fifth place, fourth place, and moved up to third place, when all of a sudden this German in lane three began to slap my left arm. I almost stopped because of the pain, but I continued to run my race. Every slap shot pain throughout my body as I went from third place to fourth place and eventually finished in fifth place.

After the race, all types of emotions ran through me. At first, I wanted to confront the other runner and pop him upside the head. But then I decided to be the better person and walk away. However, by taking fifth place, I did not advance and I was eliminated from the finals, all due to foul play by another competitor. Little did I know, though, at that moment the U.S. coaches filed a complaint and petitioned for a review of the race. The officials went back and looked at the video and saw proof that my race was impeded by the German, who intentionally and repeatedly slapped my arm. Consequently he was disqualified, and I went from fifth place to fourth place, making me eligible for the finals.

This example of how and how not to perform during a competition has stuck with me ever since. Yes, we all want to win, but winning and being a winner can be two different things. A true winner is someone who is not willing to compromise his or her principles for the sake of momentary glory. True winners are those who do not conduct themselves with unsportsmanlike behavior.

It might seem puzzling to some people that athletes get so hyped and excited over a "game." Yet any of those same people might show a similar reaction and excitement by doing their best to make sure they're close to the front of the line at a book-signing event held by a favorite author. Both scenarios display a competitive nature; the only difference is that they are in different genres.

Here are some of the questions this book will answer:

1. What kind of person overcomes the inevitable hurdles of life?
2. How do you deal with defeat when you have given all you can and still come up short?
3. How do you bounce back from defeat?
4. How do you deal with the pressures of life?
5. How do you deal with life when you don't feel loved because someone has betrayed you?

We may not like to think about these things, but they are common hurdles for many. More important, if we do not learn a way, a personal technique with which to deal with the obstacles in life, we will be defeated. Let me repeat: obstacles are inevitable, but failure is not.

The objective of this book is to help you by offering principles that have worked for me. The course of my life has taken me through painful relationships, disappointments, betrayal, and defeat. I've been tripped up and made false starts, but I've always kept my eyes on the prize. I always strive to be the kind of person who commands respect and trust. As a result, my life's path has also taken me to Olympic glory, number one rankings, and to becoming a father and an entrepreneur. I am a witness to the fact that you can bounce back. I am living proof that no matter what you are faced with, you can overcome. All you have to do is work the plan to find your zone. If you faithfully apply the principles in this book, you, too, can be the first to break the tape at your personal finish line.

OLYMPIC CHAMPION—TWICE

TEAMWORK MAKES THE DREAM WORK

"Teamwork makes the dream work." This famous saying was coined by John C. Maxwell. Regardless of how talented, rich, or blessed you are, having a team is a mandatory prerequisite for success. A good team provides support and accountability systems. However, if you are like I was, you may not have an established team in place. Most of the time, my team starts with my family. But what if your family is not around for you to depend on? And how do you build a successful team when it appears that nobody else cares about what you're striving to accomplish?

When I set out to become an Olympic champion, few people in my environment believed in and supported my goal. At first, it was quite discouraging to try to believe in myself when those close to me did not seem to support me. I recall coming home to the smells of fried pork chops, French fries, fried corn, and butter-saturated corn bread. I wanted to eat that food so badly, but to be an Olympic champion I had to maintain a strict diet, and fried food wasn't on it.

1

In order to be a champion, I had to have discipline, but the aromas made that food a strong temptation. Furthermore, when I was encouraged to eat the food anyway and teased when I declined, my resolve weakened even more. At that moment, I realized that I had to find a support system to encourage me and help me stay accountable.

Here are some steps that worked for me and helped me secure my team:

1. Identify your current environment.
2. Envision the environment you desire.
3. Begin to associate with people who are on the path to where you want to go.
4. Find ways to join forces with those people and help them with their goals.

In order to meet people like this, I had to spend even more time in the gym and on the field. I had to surround myself with successful people to learn the traits of a successful person. Hanging around athletes and coaches encouraged me to stay focused on my dream. Eventually, those athletes and coaches saw my desire and began to assist me with my goal. I recall coaches taking me out to dinner and inviting me over for a healthy meal. I eventually acquired my team by intentionally putting myself in the environment that I needed to be in to meet my goals.

If you are struggling with finding a team to help you, I suggest you spend time around people and places that represent where you want to go. Demonstrate a strong work ethic, earn the respect of others, cultivate relationships, and be willing to help others meet their dreams as well.

MARKS OF A CHAMPION

The characteristics of a champion are often a result of the marks, or the scars, that are inflicted during the process of becoming a champion. But it is those marks that remind the champion how to win and succeed. Don't be afraid to fail or lose. Failing does not make you a failure. You become a failure only when you don't get back up! No champion wins every time, and you don't have to win every time to lead a successful life. While no one always wins, no victor ever settles for being a victim. Being a victor requires an active stance. There is no place for passivity when running the race of life, and a true champion takes no joy in crushing an opponent.

ATLANTA SUMMER OLYMPIC GAMES

As the sky darkened on a southern summer evening, I could still see the five vivid colors of the Olympic rings wave over the stadium. "Sweet Georgia Brown" blared through the loudspeakers as fireworks lit the Atlanta night. It was July 19, 1996, and with nearly 11,000 athletes representing 197 different nations, I entered the Olympic Stadium for the opening ceremonies of the Centennial Games. I was now an Olympian, a privilege reserved for only a minute fraction of society—the best athletes in the world.

White curtains rose from the center of the stadium, exposing silhouettes of classic Greek athletes who performed under a faint glow. Marching bands entertained the over-flowing crowd as the traditional parade of nations began. The United States delegation circled the stadium, with me among them, waving in time to the roar of the audience caught up in the magical spell of the moment.

As we walked, many thoughts ran through my mind. I thought of all the prayers that had been said, and the love I felt from so many people. I thought about the many sacrifices I had made—from forgoing delicious chocolate chip cookies to steering clear of performance-enhancing drugs. I knew there could be no cheating in any area if I wanted to achieve my dreams. Every difficult step I had taken gave me the confidence I needed to succeed. And finally, I thought back on all those longs hours of training. It was so very tough, but it was all worth it now.

President Bill Clinton began the sixteen days of Olympic Games by officially announcing, "I declare open the Games of Atlanta, celebrating the Twenty-Sixth Olympiad of the modern era." The feeling of pride throughout the stadium was contagious as the parade continued amid the spine-tingling roar of the crowd. When it was time for the lighting of the Olympic cauldron, the crowd began to cheer wildly as they realized that Muhammad Ali had been chosen to light the flame. We all held our breath as we watched Ali, with the Olympic torch clutched tightly in his shaking left hand, attempt to light the flame. Because of his Parkinson's disease, his entire left arm shook uncontrollably as he attempted to lift the torch to the fuse. As if on cue, the crowd began to chant, "You can do it!" Ali stood there for what seemed like an eternity, arm shaking, torch in hand, struggling to reach the fuse. I could see that Ali was struggling on the inside as well as the outside, for what must have seemed to him like a very long time. Finally, he was able to lift his arm and light the fuse, and the fireball began to burn brightly over the stadium. The crowd cheered as Ali stepped down from the platform, and it was then that I understood the symbolism in that moment. It was almost as if God were saying to me, "Mark, if Ali can do it with his shaking left hand, you can do it with your broken left arm!" I felt incredibly encouraged from that moment on, and I knew that nothing was going to stop me from competing.

Because I was ranked number one in the world, my family and I received extra privileges once we arrived in Atlanta. We stayed in a beautiful suite in a downtown Atlanta hotel. This setting was reserved for the "superstars," because it was more serene and peaceful. My family tended to my two-week-old daughter, Ebony, as I began preparing my mind for battle. Chills ran through my body as I thought about the fact that I was not only representing myself at these Olympic Games, but I was also representing my race, my schools, my heritage, my country, and my God. With that in mind, I knew it was time to get in the zone.

The first thing I did was lay out my USA uniform in the reverse order from which I would put it on; sweatpants, tights, shorts, socks, and top. The next step was the spikes. I replaced the old needles with new ones and placed them right under my uniform. Once that was complete, I shut the door and entered into deep meditation and prayer. I began to visualize my race and thanked God in advance for the victory. Believe it or not, victory is determined before you get into the blocks and before you start to compete. The winner has already been chosen. The victor is the one who believes he *can* and focuses on the positive rather than the negative. I was ready and prepared, physically, mentally, and spiritually. Although my arm was hurting, I was not going to let anything stop me from competing.

My arm hurt because it was broken. Just two weeks prior to the Olympics, I decided to complete one more workout at UCLA. It was my last set, and I was fatigued going over those last few hurdles. I caught my lead leg on one of the 42-inch wooden hurdles, and as I reached out with my left arm to break my fall, I heard a crack and fell. I remember sitting on the ground in excruciating pain, waiting for it to get better. I was hoping that I had just bruised it or pulled something. But the pain wouldn't go away. When I tried to ice it, the pressure of the ice made it hurt more. I went to the doctor, who took an X-ray and then came back into the room: "Well, Mark Crear, I have some bad news," he said. "You broke your arm. You have a fractured radial head."

What?! With his even and calm demeanor, it didn't seem to me that he realized he had just crushed my big dream. I thought my bid for the Olympics was over. My whole world stopped at that moment. All the training, sacrifice, and honest dedication were for nothing? My chance to compete couldn't be over. Or could it?

But strangely enough, someone told me that he "knew a guy who knew a guy" who might be able to help me out. Later that evening, I called this man and explained what had happened. He said that he could "speed up" my recovery period and at the same time enhance my strength and speed. I was curious to know how he could perform this miracle and proceeded to listen. After a minute of idle talk, he finally said the words *anabolic steroids*. He said that he would fix things. All I had to do was give him the green light. I thanked him and said that I would call him back tomorrow. That was another crucial moment in my life. I had to decide whether I was going to cheat, give up, or fight back. I remember hearing God's still, small voice in my mind say at that moment, *Mark, you've come too far to stop now, so don't stop!* After I prayed, I heard God say again, *Mark, it isn't over until I say it's over.*

This was the first and last time I have ever been approached about illegal drugs. I have never cheated, or thought seriously about cheating for that matter, and I was not about to start now. No matter what! Having made that declaration, I called the man back and declined his offer, saying, "I am going to trust God, who is the author and finisher of my faith," and hung up.

At that moment, I told myself I was going to make it. I didn't know how, but I knew I would overcome even this high hurdle. I went back to the doctor, and he asked me if I wanted him to put my arm in a cast. I told him, "Yes, but I'd prefer a soft cast." I didn't want a full, hard cast because I didn't want my competition to know about my injury. I was all the more determined. You see, I did not know the future, but I knew who did—almighty God—and He could make a way out of *no way!*

I prayed: "Father, I want to go into this race victorious. I am not going out there doubtful. . . . I know that you have not brought me this far to leave me. . . . Thank you, Lord, in advance for this victory." I remember feeling confident and powerful. I felt anointed, and I knew that the Holy Spirit was truly in me. I danced and praised the Lord, truly thanking him. I was so confident that I was going to win a medal, I couldn't envision anything else.

But the pain in my arm was tremendous as I competed in each round that determined who would go to the finals. After placing my feet in the starting blocks, I had to position my arms in a way that put tremendous pressure on my left arm. It became obvious that my competitors knew something was wrong, because at one point during warm-ups one of the runners swung his arm around, getting too close to me on purpose and hitting me on my broken arm. Pain shot through my entire body, but I didn't say a thing. I kept focused. I was in lane eight, the far right side of the track, next to the crowd. And before I even could comprehend it, I realized that I had made the finals.

Standing behind the starting blocks of the Olympic finals—the race that would determine the medalists—I felt an intense determination within me. Allen Johnson, Colin Jackson, and Tony Jarrett were just a few of the athletes against whom I would be competing. The cheering of the crowd and the flashing cameras would not deter me from focusing on my goal.

"Runners, take your marks," said the starter.

This was it. I went into the blocks, my legs shaking from a last-minute stretch. I took in a deep breath as I tuned out the yells and gestures of the other athletes. I placed my fingers behind the shiny white start line and then placed my arms in position. The sharp pain was there, but I spoke back to it.

"Not right now," I said. Looking up at the hurdles and then placing my head back down again, I said, "Let's go get it!"

The gun went off, and we began to run. I remember so vividly seeing Allen Johnson out just a little bit in front of me. I kept saying to myself, *I can do it*. We were head-to-head at one point. Then he picked up speed and hit a hurdle. He hit another and another, and I thought I was going to pass him. I kept running and running—and although my arm was hurting and swinging wildly, I kept going. I remember going over that last hurdle and charging toward the finish line. At that moment I heard a voice say, *Well done*. I briefly closed my eyes as I crossed the finish line, and when I opened them again, I saw that Johnson had won the gold. Seconds later I heard my name: "Mark Crear, silver medal winner!"

I looked into the crowd, searching for my family. My heart pounded in my chest as the realization and joy of my victory began to sink in. I was an Olympic silver medal winner, and no one could take that from me!

SYDNEY SUMMER OLYMPIC GAMES

With 10,651 athletes competing in more than three hundred events, the Sydney 2000 Games of the Twenty-Seventh Olympiad were the largest yet. Once again, I was one of the few selected to compete in my event. I remember Sir William Deane, governor-general of Australia, opening the games to the momentous roar of the crowd. Cheers and celebration quickly turned into a focused determination as the athletes began to prepare for their competitions.

Not only was I a competitor, however; I was also a spectator. Cathy Freeman had the honor of lighting the Olympic flame at the opening ceremony of the games. As an Aboriginal medal hopeful, she had come to symbolize the desire to reconcile the white and Aboriginal populations of Australia. Ten days later, Cathy Freeman won the 400-meter finals. This clear victory took place in front of an ecstatic crowd. Birgit Fischer earned two gold medals in kayaking, to become the first woman in any sport to win medals twenty years apart. Japanese athlete Judoka Ryoko Tamura lost in the judo finals in both Barcelona and Atlanta, but later came back to win the gold medal in Sydney. Steven Redgrave from Great Britain (indoor rowing) became the first person to win gold medals at five consecutive Olympics. Fellow USA star Marion Jones (track and field) was the first woman to win five medals in athletics in the same Olympics. Unfortunately, she later tested positive for a banned substance and had to surrender her aforementioned medals.

One of the perks of being on the Olympic team was having access to the other athletes and staying at the Olympic Village. At first glance, the Olympic Village resembled a refugee camp of sorts. People from all walks of life and countries were grouped together in little "cities," all surrounded by security gates. Each country occupied a certain dormitory, which was clearly marked by its respective flag. From where I was, the Cuban flag hung to the left and to the right hung a gigantic Jamaican flag.

The cafeteria, or, as we called it, the mess hall, was located in the center of the village. McDonald's was one of the sponsors of the Olympic Games and so that was what most athletes had for lunch. There was also a station-based buffet where you could order anything from Chinese food to Mexican food. I stayed near the Italian section and ate mostly salad and spaghetti.

The cafeteria was also the designated hangout where athletes networked and made friends with athletes from other countries. The norm was to exchange Olympic gear with an athlete from a different country. I remember trading one of my USA jackets for a Japanese Olympic jacket. It was just part of the Olympic Village experience and was the highlight for many athletes. There was also a dance club and a game room for the athletes to enjoy. Many of the athletes who were finished with competing spent a lot of their time there.

But I had no time for that. One thing and one thing only was on my mind—a gold medal. It amazed me how so many athletes seemed to have focuses and objectives totally different from mine. Some athletes go to the Olympics to mainly hang out, while others are just happy to have made the team in the first place. But athletes such as Allen Johnson, Michael Johnson, Gail Devers, Marion Jones, and I came to the games to win. Nothing else would be acceptable, and failure was not an option. Our behavior was easy to distinguish because we were never seen and usually stayed outside the village in order to stay focused. There was always one barber in the group, and everyone seemed to sign up to get their hair trimmed before their race. We had been in Australia for more than three weeks, and our hair was in desperate need of a pair of clippers.

The night before the competition started, the pace slowed down. By that time I was already in my hotel room

getting ready for battle. And believe me, a battle it was! A total of 10,651 athletes were fighting for three medals in their
respective events—gold, silver, and bronze. Wow! Ready or
not . . . it's time!

I arrived at the warm-up track early the next morning. It
was also day one of the men's high hurdles competition. At
first glance, the track looked like a three-ring circus. Athletes
were throwing javelins, jumping hurdles, pole-vaulting, and
taking sprints all at the same time, all on the same track. As
I started my warm-up laps, I noticed Maurice Greene doing
sprints and Marion Jones getting a massage on her personal
trainer's table. While they were getting ready to race, I was
trying to digest and comprehend the fact that I had a double
hernia.

It had to have happened during one particular workout,
but it was only in hindsight that I understood what went
wrong. About two weeks prior, I was doing strength speed
training, which consisted of my pulling a sled with one
hundred pounds attached to it. I remember straining as I
squeezed out every ounce of energy I could. As I pressed forward for the last ten yards, I felt a slight pinch in my groin,
but I had only yards to go and I was not about to stop. With
just two more yards, I felt another pinch in my hip flexor
area. One yard to go, and then I crossed the finish line. I
was ready to compete! Later that day I felt a continual sharp
pain in my hip flexor area every time I coughed, laughed, or
made any sudden movement. I thought it was just fatigue,
so I proceeded to ice it and get my physical therapy—deep
tissue massage. In retrospect that deep tissue massage actually irritated and tore open the wound even more. But not

knowing that, every time the pain occurred, I got more deep tissue massages, causing greater harm to my body.

Finally, it occurred to me that it had to be a double hernia. Upon arriving at the Olympic training village, I saw a doctor, who suggested an MRI. Once the report was back, it confirmed that I had a double hernia and needed immediate surgery. But as far as I was concerned, it was just another hurdle that I would have to face. Surgery just two days prior to my competition was not an option. So I leaned on my faith once more and on my past Olympic experience to get me through.

"What's up, Crear?" Michael Johnson asked as I ran past him, trying my best to hide any sign of pain. Showing signs of weakness and injury at the Olympics was a no-no. At that point in the game, it's mental.

When I arrived at the warm-up hurdle area, I was anxious to start my routine. It usually takes me an hour to an hour and a half to warm up and be ready to run. I noticed that the "pecking order" and the fight for priority space was already under way. I picked my lane and hurdles and set them up accordingly. I did not like other athletes using or going over my hurdles. That is an unwritten law among hurdlers. Space was the name of the game, and I demanded mine. If someone needed a hurdle, too bad . . . they could go somewhere else. It may sound hard, but those are the rules. Everyone has their own routine, and no one likes interference.

Once I was ready, I headed for the main stadium. Before entering the holding area, the media greeted us. I remember Terrence Trammell saying as he passed the camera, "Hi, Mom. I love you." At that moment a wave of displaced nerves, emotions, and sadness swept through my heart. I had heard so many athletes through the years make the same declaration of love, yet I had never even mouthed *Hello, Mom*, while looking at the cameras. It was then that I realized I had never once told my dad that I loved him either. Those precious memories that so many take for granted: playing catch with their dads, sitting together as a family at the dinner table—I don't have them. My life was different.

I then began to focus on some of my family's recent behavior, and this, too, began to weigh heavily on my heart. *Why me?* I wondered. *What did I do that was so wrong?* In a matter of seconds, I went from feeling good to feeling depressed and defeated. Not a good place to be before competing in a race.

"Excuse me," said one of the security guards. "May I have your autograph? I just wanted to let you know that you are a great inspiration to me, and I'm a huge fan." At that moment I snapped back into reality, and as quickly as the depression had come over me, it was gone. I thanked him and felt on top of the world once again. I was ready to race. That man will never know what a gift he gave me.

Here I was again. My second Olympics, and I was standing behind the blocks in the finals. Once again, I had an injury that I had to block out. And yes, once again, I had to bear the nauseating smell of Bengay accentuated with sweat. "Thirty seconds," said a man from the television crew as he walked past each lane, followed by the camera. All I could hear were scrambled sounds of cheering and clapping. The flashes from the spectators' cameras made it difficult to see. And then, all at once, it became ghostly quiet. The starter said, "Runners, take your marks." I took in a deep breath and tucked myself into the blocks, like a bow and arrow waiting to be fired.

Bang! Bang! I shot out of the blocks like a rocket. "False start!" said the starter.

This was serious. At this point I didn't have anything else left. I could barely walk back to the starting blocks without clenching in pain. I began to speak to God. "God, I know that you brought me here for a reason . . . so let's go." And then I felt peace once again.

"Wait for the gun," warned the starter. "Runners, take your marks."

Bang! This time there was no false start, and we were off and running. *One, two, three, four, five, six, seven, eight, AT-TACK!* Over the first hurdle I went. When I looked up, I was at least two steps behind. I had gotten a terrible start because of the pain, but I kept running and running. Every time I went over a hurdle I said to myself, *I can do it! I can do it!*

I saw Anier Garcia and Terrence Trammell to my left, but nobody to my right. *Whack!* I hit the fourth hurdle and it pushed me farther behind, but I kept going. I kept digging, fighting, running and running. Suddenly, I began to see my entire life as a race— running *from* my classmates as a child, running *from* my father, running *from* danger. *Not anymore, no more running from*, I thought and ran even faster.

As I went over the last hurdle, my vision changed. All I could think of was running to . . . running *to* a happy future . . . running *to* victory. And I was determined to get there. *Lean!* I said to myself as Allen Johnson and I crossed the finish line in unison. Garcia won the gold and Trammel clearly

15

won the silver. After about 30 seconds, as we waited to see who had won the bronze, my name popped up on the big screen: Crear—Olympic bronze medal.

I was so excited! I jumped for joy and ran over to where my daughter, Ebony, was sitting. I looked at her and gave her a wink. "We did it again," I said as I scooped her up for a second consecutive victory lap. Cameras flashed as the crowd cheered. It did not matter who came in first because, for me, my bronze was gold.

HURDLES AND OBSTACLES

Imagine yourself driving down the road of life—beautiful blossoming apple trees are everywhere, but lightning causes one to fall across the road. You screech to a halt. How do you get over this obstacle and get to your destination? Many people might say, "Just find a way to get over it." But the question is How? Being a two-time Olympic champion, I've been faced with many hurdles and obstacles to overcome. Some were on the competition field, yet most were not. It's easy to see the end results, but many people don't see what it took to get there. *People may see the glory, but they don't know the story.*

We all face tough challenges in life. Some are difficult to overcome, especially when the odds are stacked against us. Yet going against all odds is something we're capable of doing. To overcome challenges, you need to have a method and a plan to bounce back and succeed.

Success requires great planning and even greater effort. From business success to personal achievement, the potential for success is in direct proportion to the way you deal with painful things and the inevitable obstacles that come into your life. The key word here is *inevitable*. We are inevitably going to be faced with obstacles, disappointments, and pain. It is how we respond to each accordingly that makes some of us successful while others flounder.

PAIN IS INEVITABLE, BUT SUFFERING IS AN OPTION

Many suffer needlessly and waste priceless years because of obstacles they are unable to overcome. In part due to the fact that I was a runner who won two Olympic medals, I've endured great losses and achieved many successes. There is a story behind every successful person. Every successful person has been faced with hurdles, major obstacles, defeat, rejection, and betrayal. The common denominator among successful people, however, is their ability to overcome those hurdles, regain momentum, and bounce back to finish the race.

In order to overcome, one must have a plan. As the saying goes, "If you fail to plan, then you plan to fail." You need a method and a course of action to get over, through, and beyond the hurdle or obstacle you're facing. Successful people know this. It doesn't take rocket science, but it might take a little help from a coach or reading a book like this one.

STAGES OF HURDLING

During my time as a world-class hurdler, I realized the similarity between running the hurdles in the Olympics and overcoming the hurdles in life. Briefly, here is a track-and-field clinic on how to effectively run a hurdle race. After seeing how to effectively hurdle, I'm sure you will see the similarities between the hurdles we face on the track and the ones we face off the track.

Before attempting to do anything, knowing how to do it right is highly recommended. In the process of learning, a runner also learns a certain technique. Applying this technique is the key to improvement. And in the athletic world, technique is the form and method we use to jump the hurdles. Likewise, in life it is crucial that we discover a formula and technique to overcome obstacles that block our paths. There are three stages to hurdling.

First Stage: Take Off

This is the beginning, where we take off or use power to push into the hurdle, or, as a runner calls it, to "attack" the hurdle. This first phase is important because it sets the momentum and power necessary to get over the hurdle. Likewise in life, how you start is equally important. Allowing yourself enough power and momentum in the beginning is essential to achieving your goal. There's a saying that it doesn't matter how you start, just how you finish. Just as in a race, one does not want to start the race of life from the back of the pack. Understand that in life, just like a race, your start is important because it prepares you for the second stage, which is balance.

Second Stage: Position and Balance

Being in the correct position and having the correct balance over the hurdle is essential for coming off the hurdle and not stumbling. So once we push off, we have to make sure that we are positioned accurately over the hurdle by leaning not to the left or to the right, but from the middle, and having our center of gravity balanced in our body position, which is parallel to the ground.

In life, the same principle applies. Putting yourself in a position of balance reduces your chances of tripping and falling. Balance also prevents you from getting off-focus and distracted. Balance is a key ingredient in the lives of successful people. Being aware of your position and balancing will help you rebound and recover from whatever you're going through. And once you have your balance, you can handle more weight without feeling overwhelmed. Likewise, balance helps you feel in control and positions you to take advantage of your momentum.

Third Stage: Running Off

This is our ending phase, which is the running off of the hurdle. Once a hurdler touches the ground, he or she is "running off" the hurdle, leaving it behind. This phrase is important because it moves us forward and into preparing to jump the next hurdle. Once we've established a solid takeoff, followed by gaining the balance necessary to run and stay on course, it's time to leave the last hurdle behind and run to the finish line. The goal is to cross the finish line and complete the task at hand. This third phase is crucial to our success. It's that running to the finish line, reaching, stretching, and enduring to the end. And remember that a runner is not running *away* from the hurdle but is always focused on running *toward* the finish. In life, it's important to remember that if you think about what's behind you, you are not focused on what counts. What counts is moving toward your goals.

BEGINNING THE PROCESS

My people are destroyed for lack of knowledge. (Hosea 4:6 KJV)

The first step in overcoming your obstacles or hurdles is to be aware and acknowledge that you have hurdles to overcome. Being able to identify your hurdles is the next crucial step to overcoming them. Many of us have problems and are faced with great challenges but rarely take the time to identify those challenges. If we don't name our challenges, they retain their power over us and continue to linger in our lives. They breed in the dark of our ignorance.

If you are wondering if you are facing hurdles, here are some symptoms:

- Stress
- Anxiety
- Depression
- Doubt
- Fear
- Loneliness
- Despair
- Hopelessness
- Just going through the motions of life
- Rationalizing
- Compromising principles

- Sleeplessness
- Lack of self-control

If you have stopped dreaming, stopped believing, stopped trying, or stopped caring, you are in trouble. If you are feeling any of the above, then you are more than likely faced with some obstacles and hurdles in your life. The good news is that there is hope. You can overcome these hurdles and succeed, and you are not alone. And the greatest news is: God will never leave you or forget about you.

PHYSICAL, MENTAL, AND SPIRITUAL HURDLES

Many people are oblivious to the hurdles they are facing on a daily basis, and they do not understand what causes their symptoms. Any of us at any time can encounter many different types of hurdles. Here are a few types of hurdles that plague a lot of people, perhaps even you.

Hurdles We Create for Ourselves

This is a hurdle that everyone experiences to some degree in his or her life. Sometimes we are our own biggest enemies. Yes, we are the problem. We are in our own way, hindering our own growth, and stopping our own progress. This means we are self-sabotaging our own success, sometimes without even knowing it. Many people who come into my office for help suffer from this very thing: the young man who never seems to be able to fully commit in a relationship, the married couple who always start fighting just before they want to have a serious conversation, the executive who makes an inappropriate joke in front of his boss just before his annual review. These are examples of self-defeating behavior. We all do it, but if it becomes so commonplace in your life that you just can't help yourself, you may need to see someone who can help you name and get over that hurdle.

Without being properly identified, our problems will cause us to unconsciously defeat ourselves even before we begin. Upon identification of a problem, fighting the associated anxiety, depression, or rejection can still be a challenging and daunting task. In my own life I have experienced a great deal of self-destructive behavior and low self-esteem. I beat myself up and placed my own hurdles in front of me. It's difficult to find the finish line when you are constantly running off the track to set another obstacle that needs to be hurdled. Be fully aware that self-hurdles can cause us to fail, and it is altogether possible that they can also rob us of our ability to get back up. The object is for us to speak life to ourselves. If you find yourself talking about yourself in a negative way, downplaying your abilities, making yourself the butt of jokes, or even harshly criticizing what you do, then you are struggling with self-hurdles and will find yourself feeling dissatisfied and defeated.

Hurdles Resulting from Pressure

The pressure to perform; the demand to compete, win, succeed, meet quotas; and many other societal expectations are major hurdles that we face daily. Whether you're an athlete faced with the challenges of flawlessly competing, a student faced with the pressure of getting all As to keep that scholarship, or an employee faced with closing the deal on a major account, pressures, expectations, and demands can be difficult to manage. Many of us face these hurdles without having a formula to deal with the pressure, resulting in choking, underachieving, or just giving in to defeat. Formulating your own method of dealing with the pressure of competition and high expectations is crucial to your success.

Financial Hurdles

During these slow economic times, who doesn't face these hurdles? They can exist in the forms of being laid off, short- or long-term unemployment, bankruptcy, not being able to pay your bills, not being able to afford college, and lacking sufficient necessities. Financial hurdles can appear in the life of anyone and everyone, regardless of race, religion, or nationality. Financial hurdles are a major reason that marriages break up. Learning how to deal with financial hardships and prioritizing how you spend money is crucial for your success.

Spiritual Hurdles

These are the challenges that we face in our spiritual walks. Some of us may be challenged in our belief and faith in God. Some of us may have been wronged or betrayed by spiritual leaders. Church members or the church itself may have betrayed and harmed you. When the place where you expected to find peace, grace, forgiveness, and mercy fails you or puts you down, this can amount to a major hurdle. Also, when your faith and belief in God are weak or you feel that God has let you down; when you feel that your prayers have not been answered; when you feel that you've done everything according to God's way but harm, disappointment, and pain still cross your path; when you see the hypocrites prospering while you are trying so hard to do the right thing—all these can be hurdles to you. Having peace with your God is imperative to having peace in your life.

Societal Hurdles

Have you ever felt that you don't fit in? How about the feeling that you're not good enough? Are you are too big, too skinny, too tall, too short, too light, too dark, too smart, or too dumb? When society has its own clique and you do not fit in, that's a societal hurdle. Almost everyone wants to feel that they are a part of something greater than themselves. Almost everybody wants to feel that they belong, but there are cases where no matter what you do, no matter what you try, you do not seem to fit into the mainstream societal culture.

Understanding who you are and whose you are is crucial for overcoming societal hurdles and succeeding in reaching your goals. Society should not be your judge; God and you should be your judges. The ability to define yourself and not let society define you is crucial to your personal satisfaction and personal success. Like the late rapper Tupac Shakur often said, "Only God can judge me."

Legal Hurdles

Sometimes the "system" fails, and justice is not just. When this happens, long-lasting and regrettable ramifications often result. Instead of being considered innocent until proved guilty, you might look guilty to the powers that be and have the unpleasant and challenging task of proving yourself innocent. Factor in racial and cultural discrimination and bias, along with the various forms of profiling, and the justice system becomes a hurdle rather than a bridge to a better life.

Regardless of whether you were falsely accused or are guilty of committing an illegal act, recovering from legal hurdles is challenging, costly, and time-consuming. Knowing that the ultimate Judge—God—loves us and will intercede on our behalf is reassuring but may not provide immediate relief.

Relationship Hurdles

There is nothing more painful and emotionally draining than a divorce or the breakup of a relationship. Dealing with attorneys, courts, paperwork, custody battles, property battles; challenging those character accusations, custody evaluations, documentations; and the reality of a broken home is devastating. Members of divorced families face alienation from one another, having their characters and good names assassinated. It is no wonder that divorce is the number one hurdle many of us face, and we all know of someone who has faced or is facing this obstacle.

Knowing that we are capable of repairing and rebuilding our lives is essential for our future growth and development.

Knowing that whatever is taken from us will be replaced with something better, knowing that whatever heartache we are facing, God will help us, aids in the healing process. But the wounds take time to heal, and we may be living with a limp for a long time.

Hurdles of Abuse

Abuse can be a silent killer. This hurdle affects too many people, myself included. When we say "abuse," most of us think of violence of some kind. But there are abusive acts beyond violence. True, violence is one form of abuse, but abuse also can have emotional, verbal, financial, and social components. Bullying—at home, school, or the workplace— is an example. How you deal with these abusive hurdles will frame how you deal with the rest of your life. Finding not only the strength to change your heart and mind but the courage to address and stop the abuse is necessary in regaining confidence, security, and peace of mind.

Dealing with abusive obstacles is difficult. Most abuse comes from individuals we want to trust: a parent, sibling, brother or sister, mother or father, husband or wife, teacher, coach, employer, or even a member of the clergy. It is challenging to deal with the reality when the ones we trust, the ones in whom we put our faith, are, in fact, abusers. Whom do we turn to when those who are supposed to be there for us in times of trouble are the ones we fear?

I witnessed and suffered firsthand the ramifications of being in an abusive environment. I recall many times when I was afraid to speak up for fear of getting hit or being yelled at. I recall the heavy burden of keeping up appearances so I could be accepted by society; yet behind closed doors, I lived in chaos, violence, and dysfunction. A person who has been or is being abused often fears opening up to others, feeling embarrassment and anticipating a lack of understanding.

Abuse is not just something that *happens to* a person. Abuse destroys personhood and possibilities for future health and well-being. The younger the person is who experiences abuse, the more likely it is that he or she will suffer irreversible consequences. Some hurdles are too high. Some wounds are so deep they leave scars that disfigure and distort the personality. Healing and recovery from being in a violent and abusive environment requires a forgiving and adaptable spirit. I made it through mine, so I know it's not impossible. Don't give up and don't give in. Instead, grab hold of your life with an unshakable grip. You can and will overcome this hurdle.

Hurdles of Insecurity and Codependency

These hurdles are kin to loneliness and abandonment. Many of us are consumed with feeling all alone, even in a room full of people. These are difficult obstacles to overcome, especially when we feel that there is no one who truly cares. Maybe you see yourself as "different." Maybe people have made fun of you. Maybe people just do not "get" you. Because we all have flaws, most everyone is laughed at, picked on, and talked about at some time, but for many people the way they've been treated is debilitating, resulting in their becoming loners and withdrawing from society.

The need to be wanted, to just be accepted and loved, is basic to human beings, innate within all of us. All most people ever want is a kind word, someone to love them, and someone they can love. Unfortunately, along the path, we encounter hurdles that frustrate this need.

Hurdles of Betrayal

Have you ever been lied to, backstabbed, cheated on, or, as we say, "played"? If you answered yes, then you have faced this type of hurdle. There's nothing more painful than being betrayed by someone whom you considered a friend, whether a family member, an associate, a classmate, an authority figure, or a colleague. Betrayal hurdles are very painful and difficult to get over. Most of us have experienced or will experience the challenging task of overcoming betrayal hurdles. Some of you may be experiencing one or a combination of betrayal hurdles, even at this moment as you read this book.

The good news is that you can recover from betrayal. The good news is that no weapon formed against you shall prosper. The good news is that whatever was taken can be replaced with something even better. The one thing that no one can take away from you is you, your principles and your morals.

Hurdles of Addiction

There are few things as terrifying as addiction for an individual or family. While alcohol is the leading cause of divorce, right behind it are financial stressors. But in these cases alcohol addiction is common. No matter the drug of choice, addiction is a crippling hurdle. Many of us know someone who has suffered from some type of addiction and others who are currently struggling with addiction hurdles in their lives.

There are many types of addiction other than those involving drugs and alcohol. Even though addictions to such things as shopping, working, gambling, and pornography are not necessarily deemed by society as dangerous, they can be just as destructive.

WHY ME?

After naming their personal hurdles, people begin to ask Why? Why is this happening to me? How could this happen to me? Taking an honest look at yourself and your situation can help answer the question why. Identifying your participation, your accountability, and your responsibility for the hurdle is the next step toward healing.

Next we must understand and accept that sometimes bad things do happen to good people. In many cases, the hurdles in our lives are caused by other people's hurdles and insecurities getting in our way or other people putting their hurdles in our lane. As Joyce Meyer says, "Hurting people hurt people."

However, regardless of the who or why behind your hurdle, being able to identify the hurdle and an applicable solution is the key to getting over and overcoming it. Regardless of what your hurdles are, you will recover. All you have to do is get back up one more time, no matter which hurdle knocks you down.

Now what? That is the million-dollar question. After we have discovered and named the hurdles that we face and found our way over them, then what? We live in a society that is quick to scrutinize and exploit errors; yet it offers little, if any, real solutions to the problems. To elaborate, many parents criticize and punish their kids for wrongdoing, but more often than not, they don't provide a solution for cleaning up the mess. It is one thing to yell and cry over spilled milk; it is quite another thing to provide the paper towels to clean up the spill.

Throughout my years as a world-class Olympian hurdler, Christian counselor, divorced husband, and proud father, I have made many mistakes and been attacked countless times. If I had only known then what I know now, I would have been able to overcome those hurdles without experiencing prolonged agony, suffering, and financial hardship.

PURPOSE

Being in the zone helped me beat obstacles and race to Olympic medals. This chapter will begin to explore the training strategies and principles that worked for me and can work for you. It's all about finding, getting, and staying in the zone that will lead to success despite inevitable hurdles. In the zone, performance training consists of a dynamic six-step action plan designed to assist individuals, companies, and organizations successfully meet their objectives. The program is made up of the six Ps: purpose, preparation, passion, permission, prayer, and practice.

Many athletes and professionals use the term "zone" to describe a place of consistent execution and excellence. The phrase "in the zone" is symbolic for successful athletes and professionals. But no matter how you understand the term, when you are in the zone, you are unbeatable.

During my years as a professional Olympic athlete, there were times when I felt unbeatable and other days when I simply felt defeated. Physically, I was fine, but mentally, I was inconsistent. I realized that to be number one and stay number one, my total performance had to be consistent. That state of consistent excellence is what I refer to as being "in the zone."

We all have the desire to be in the zone. We all have the desire to be unstoppable. Many of us have watched sports performances where we saw athletes take over a game and will themselves to victory. Many of us have cheered for Michael Jordan as we witnessed firsthand what being in the zone truly is. The following steps will guide you and provide you with the tools necessary to create your personal "in the zone" blueprint. But beware: even if one athlete is in the zone and succeeds, the team can still lose the game. A culture of training and implementation of these principles is required, so everyone on your team can consistently perform at a maximum level.

The word *purpose* has been explored and discussed and defined thousands of times, spanning decades. Pastors, psychologists, and self-help gurus of all types have offered their opinions on this topic. There are many well-known books on the subject. Rick Warren's *The Purpose-Driven Life* and *How to Fulfill Your Purpose* are just two of the many. But even with all the literature and opinions about purpose, people still struggle with finding and knowing their own purposes.

While there are plenty of people telling you what purpose is, there are few who can show you how purpose can get you in the zone and succeed in reaching your daily and long-term goals. When I speak of the word *purpose*, I mean something that will answer the question "What?" Meaning that when you understand and find your purpose, it answers the question, "What am I doing?" We don't just have one purpose in life. During the course of our lives, we have multiple purposes. One of the issues that many struggle with is the notion that we each have only one purpose, and that purpose is placed in us at birth and carried with us throughout our lives. That may be correct in part, but it is not totally accurate.

I believe that we encounter several stages in life, and within each stage we each will have a specific purpose. Likewise, I believe that a person can have several purposes during the course of his or her life. It is safe to say that when you finish one purpose, you will be given another purpose to fulfill. Whether you're a Christian or not, understanding your purpose is also connected with understanding your Creator—your higher power. To find what your purpose is, all you have to do is look in the mirror. **Your purpose is you.** But this does not mean that your purpose in life is selfish desire and fulfillment, or that you are somehow a god. Rather, it's about your fruit. Here are three perspectives on purpose that will help you discover yours.

YOUR ACTIONS DETERMINE AND DEFINE YOUR PURPOSE

Many believe that your purpose will find you out. In fact, they are correct; your purpose will indeed find you out, but *based on your actions*. In essence, your actions will determine and, most of the time, reveal and define your purpose. Jesus tells us that we can tell a tree by its fruit (see Matthew 7:17-20). In the literal sense, if we are walking through the woods and come across several apples scattered around a tree, chances are good that it's an apple tree. And if we look up at that tree and see apples attached to the branches of the tree, we have proof positive that it is an apple tree. The same applies when you look at someone's character, demeanor, ethics, and attitude, which provide clues to what that person believes. For example, if you heard someone using foul language and totally disrespecting others to the point of abuse and public humiliation, you would conclude that this person had a mean-spirited character and problems with self-control. What we do helps to define our purpose. Instead of searching for purpose, we need to understand that purpose is nothing we have to search for, no more than we have to wonder if an apple is fruit of the apple tree. The fruits of our labor, or our actions, will inevitably dictate our purpose.

MANY PURPOSES

Expanding on the analogy of the apple tree can also help us see that people have not one but many purposes in life. The misperception is that we have only one purpose, and thus many of us are searching for the sole purpose and calling in our lives. The problem with that is, we were created for more than one purpose. Let me state for the record, however, that these additional purposes are independent of our spiritual connection with Christ regarding the mandates and commandments given to us by our Lord and Savior. When I suggest that we have several purposes, I am speaking with the understanding that, as Christians, we've already acknowledged our overarching purpose in Christ.

Let's say that you are the tree and the apples are your purposes. These are not for yourself, but rather for those who encounter you or those whom you encounter. An apple left on the tree too long will become spoiled. It is imperative that we give the fruit of the tree as an offering to someone else, which in turn may have perpetual results.

One passerby might see an apple, pick it up, and eat it in a spontaneous act that provides nourishment to that person. Another person might see the apple, take it home, and use it in a fresh-fruit centerpiece. Yet another might see the apple, gather several of them, and give them to someone else who is in need of food. Yet another might choose to use the apples to make an apple pie or sauce or perhaps apple juice. Regardless of the apple's intended use, the fact is that you have several apples, or purposes, that can be utilized in many different ways.

But many people believe their fruit is not worth using. They believe they don't have any talent at all or what they do have is not good enough. Like the apple tree, everything and everyone has a purpose that can be used for the good of others. Let's say you are the tree, but in this season of your life, you are not producing fruit. Yet you have a purpose, and it will be fulfilled through your actions. A passerby comes upon you, the tree, and notices there's no fruit. You may not have fruit, but you have plenty of leaves and branches to provide shade, which is just what the passerby needs to escape the hot glare of the sun. You might not provide apples but you can provide shade, which means you are still fulfilling your purpose.

SEASONAL PURPOSE

Your purpose also depends on your season of life. Just like seasons of the year, there are seasons of life that determine your purpose. Many of us compare and confuse someone else's season with the season we are in and become frustrated because we are not bearing the same fruit that someone else is. It is important to understand what season you are in. A tree does not produce fruit year-round. As there is a season for growing, there is also a time for harvesting. Regardless of what season you are in, you have a purpose, even though you might not necessarily be aware of it.

When I was in middle school, I had a friend named Ted (not his real name) who was teased a lot due to his size. Kids called him "Porky Pig" and "Fat Albert." Needless to say, Ted was a little overweight. I used to call Ted the cookie monster because nearly every time I saw him, he was eating a cookie. Not just ordinary cookies either, but home-baked cookies that he made himself: chocolate chip, sugar, oatmeal raisin, and my favorite, chocolate chip walnut cookies. I loved to spend the night at Ted's house and eat his homemade cookies. This trend continued well into his high school years, and he continued to get teased about his size and eating, but he also continued to bake homemade cookies. When everyone else was outside playing, Ted was cooking. As far as I was concerned, it worked out well, because after a hard game of basketball, I looked forward to going over to Ted's house.

Little did I know, however, that Ted was fulfilling and perfecting his purpose, which was to be a chef. Soon after high school he was discovered by a restaurateur, who hired him to be the head bakery chef at his Italian restaurant. It was just a matter of time before Ted grew in notoriety and opened his own cookie-baking business. Fast-forward, and today Ted is the CEO of a multimillion-dollar cookie company. When asked how he knew that he was going to be a baker, Ted simply replied, "I didn't. It's just what I did. I always enjoyed baking cookies, and I just did what I enjoyed." Ted was just doing what came naturally to him; and by doing that, he fulfilled his purpose to be a chef.

Do not compare your purpose with those of others. Your zone doesn't have to be similar to someone else's for you to succeed. If you are living according to the principles of Christ and, simply put, being yourself, your actions will produce your purpose. Much of the time, a person does not immediately recognize his or her purpose. Rather, the purpose is seen, felt, shared, and utilized by those around the person.

When you understand that your purpose is not something that you have to find but rather something that comes naturally to you, you will begin to realize success and fulfillment.

YOU DID THAT ON PURPOSE

We're all familiar with the statement "You did that on purpose." Anything we do is "on purpose," unless we are intoxicated or under the influence of a controlled substance, but even then we bear responsibility. Generally speaking, we are in control of our actions and choices; therefore, we must maintain accountability for them. For example, imagine that a young man states that his purpose is to become an engineer and his goal is to graduate at the top of his class. However, he signs up for the necessary classes but does not declare engineering as his major. Then he skips classes and fails the final exams. It was unrealistic for the student to expect to become an engineer after graduating at the top of his class when his actions could lead only to failure. Again, your actions dictate your purpose, not the other way around.

The first step toward tapping into your full potential and succeeding in life is to be fully aware of your actions. More than any prophecy, vision, or amount of faith you may have, without works your purpose is dead. Once you tap into your purpose, then you can answer the question What am I doing? Based on your actions, you will feel a sense of power and passion that will assist you in continuing to be productive.

There's a difference between your purpose and a goal or an objective. Your purpose answers the question: What am I on this earth to do? For example, my purpose is to encourage people to live abundant lives and, most important, to love themselves. I go through a number of steps to fulfill that purpose with joy, including motivational and inspirational speaking, life coaching, and also business coaching. One's purpose is larger than one's goal. Purpose and goal are similar and are interlinked, which might initially make it difficult to see the difference between the two. However, one of the main differences between one's purpose and goals can be found in priority and time factor. People attempt to reach their goals by setting a deadline. On the other hand, deadlines are not applicable in a purpose. A goal is the point one wishes to achieve. On the other hand, purpose can be the reason one aims to achieve a goal. Unlike purposes, goals always go forward in a specific direction. Meaning, you can and should have more goals than purposes. Thus, one's purpose is usually the sum of one's goals.

When I talk to businesses, whether they're start-ups or established, I advise them that their purpose needs to be crisp and clearly understood. Companies need to know why they're in business in the first place. They need to be clear on where their businesses are headed and what they want out of them. Being able to clearly see a company's defining purpose through business goals or a mission statement is often key for prospective lenders or investors, who are looking for success potential in a business relationship.

Serving through your purpose is optimal, but then, as you round a bend in the road, out of nowhere an obstacle blocks your path. Now what?

PREPARATION: FAITH, FOCUS, AND FORGIVENESS

Some of life's hurdles seem to appear out of nowhere, but others we can see looming in the distance. In addition, most of us have been in the race long enough that we know even if we don't see the obstacles, more than likely there is at least one around the next curve.

This chapter is about preparing for life's obstacles, which, in my experience, is best accomplished through faith, focus, and forgiveness.

FAITH

Faith is a word we use and act upon every day, but most of the time in only a general sense. You have faith that the gas station will be there when you need to fill up your car. You have faith in your colleagues and in your spouse. You might even have faith that given tough choices, you will make the right call. *Faith* is a word used and tossed around more than a basketball during a scrimmage. If you ask five different

43

people, you will get five different definitions of *faith*. The word *faith* is used not only by the spiritual or religious but by nonbelievers as well. With this word being used by so many different people in so many different ways, it can be confusing to truly understand what faith is and to realize its power and identify its source.

Faith of Believers and Nonbelievers

According to *Merriam-Webster's Dictionary, faith* is "firm belief in something for which there is no proof; complete trust." It is something that is "believed especially with strong conviction," and it is "fidelity to one's promises." Difficult to explain but powerful when experienced, Jesus said that faith can move mountains (see Matthew 17:20).

We all have faith. It doesn't matter whether we are believers or nonbelievers. The term "believers" usually connotes those who owe allegiance or have faith in a particular religious doctrine, which often centers on God and our relationship to the Divine. But, as previously mentioned, people can have faith in almost anything.

The Christian faith is not something that is applied only when necessary, in the way you would use a tube of Chap-Stick as needed for dry lips. Instead, faith is an ongoing and continuous state of being.

Faith does not promise that we will not be faced with hard times; it just reassures us that we have resources to deal with them. Faith does not guarantee that we won't be attacked; however, our faith reassures us that with God's help, we are able to defeat whatever challenges you encounter.

Faith reminds us that we are not alone. For many it points to a power higher than ourselves, someone who gives our lives purpose and meaning. The Christian faith reminds us that we have a Savior who has the power to cast down and cast out any circumstances we face. Faith reminds us that no matter what, God is with us; and nothing can separate us from God's love. Faith reminds us that we are part of a body of believers.

To prepare ourselves for any challenge, we must first have faith. Faith comes before the challenge. Likewise, faith is not determined by the outcome but is already at work before the outcome. Faith is more than a piece of our spiritual equipment; it is something that we wear continually. We have a better chance to win the race if we wear our faith comfortably and well beforehand as well as during. It is a difficult task to apply faith only after you are hurting, scared, or being attacked. A person who is startled will flinch—defensively close his or her body posture. It's harder in that position to be open and try new things, even if it's a faith that promises relief.

While it is easy to let doubts seep in when bad things happen, it is especially at those times that we have to lean on others in our faith community. That is another thing about religious faith: you can never have it alone. Be encouraged and confident. Try not to allow your obstacles to cause you to lose faith. Because at your deepest level, faith puts you in contact with all power in heaven *and* earth. Faith is not a temporary suspension of reason; rather, faith is beyond the reach of logic. Just as God is beyond us and God's ways are not ours, faith is beyond reason.

A multitude of research results have suggested that religious practices foster a sense of well-being and strengthen us. People who are part of a faith community tend to be happier, healthier, and live longer; and a healthy spirituality also encourages meaningful self-exploration, meditation, and other spiritual disciplines (e.g., prayer, study, acts of mercy and justice, fasting, worship) that can go a long way in shoring up self-confidence and building a faith that can withstand life's onslaughts. Faith is something that can grow; and as our faith grows, our relationship with God can bear much fruit.

My Personal Testimony of Faith

My perspective and position on faith is that it is a relevant and necessary element in succeeding and overcoming obstacles and hurdles in life. I am a man of faith and a Christian by confession. But even if you are not a Christian, I hope that you will be open to understanding how my faith helped me overcome painful hurdles and succeed in the midst of challenges.

Faith is to many like water is to a fish. The fish cannot see the water, but it needs the water to survive. The fish simply takes the water for granted, but without the water, the fish can survive for only so many minutes. Likewise, my faith is all around me. I am swimming, so to speak, in faith. Like the fish, I cannot see faith and don't recognize its importance until it's gone. When my faith is absent, however, I experience anxiety, pressure, depression, and disparity. Healthy fish need water, and spiritually healthy human beings need faith.

The Bible tells us that faith without works is dead, meaning that faith must be exercised. If not reinforced with corresponding behaviors, faith will simply dry up. Working our faith is something that we need to do on a daily basis. Faith is an important key element in preparing for being in the zone.

An excellent way to understand the meaning of working faith is to consider the examples of the Bible—men and women who trusted and obeyed God, placing their lives in His hands. Who were they, and what can we learn from them? Matthew 8 contains two excellent examples of faith. First, a leper was healed after saying to Jesus,

> Lord, if You are willing, You can make me clean. And, behold, there came a leper and worshipped him, saying, Lord if thou wilt, thou canst make me clean. And Jesus put forth his hand, and touched him, saying, I will; be thou clean. And immediately his leprosy was cleansed. (Matthew 8:2-3 KJV)

In another case, Christ offered to go to a Roman officer's home and heal his servant. The officer's faith in Christ's healing power was so strong that he knew Jesus didn't have to be physically present for the servant to be healed. "Lord, I am not worthy to have you come under my roof; but only speak a word, and my servant will be healed," he told Jesus (verse 8). The centurion's faith impressed Jesus so much that He said,

> I say to you with all seriousness that even in Israel I haven't found faith like this. . . . Go; it will be done for you just as you have believed. (verses 10-13).

The officer's servant immediately recovered.

On a personal note, I recall the summer of 2012 when my faith walk was put to the test. It was when I was in consideration for a speaking event with a Fortune 500 company. I was one of two candidates that had been selected for consideration. The final criteria required us to perform an in-person 5-minute sample of our keynote speech. On the surface, no problem, you might think. However, the location was in Washington, DC, and I live in Los Angeles. On top of that, we were supposed to provide our own transportation there. Well, the ticket from Los Angeles to Washington, DC, was $1,250.00. At the time, that's all I had for the remaining summer. I was confronted with the choice of spending all my money to fly to Washington for an opportunity that was not a guarantee or pass on the engagement and look elsewhere.

Talking about stepping out and walking in faith. Even though there was no guarantee that I would be the chosen speaker and I could possibly spend all my money on a trip and come back broke, I decided to step out on faith and go. I had to walk in the faith that brought me there in the first place. Wow! Was I glad I did, because not only did I get that engagement but I was immediately booked for three more.

Faith Helps Even If We Don't Understand

One of the first questions people ask when they are faced with terrible obstacles and difficult hurdles is Why is this happening? Immediately upon encountering obstacles, people try to make sense of their dilemma. They might look at their own behavior or interactions with other people as they search in their minds for the last person they were rude to or offended. When most people are confronted with a bad situation, they tend to believe it's because of something they did to deserve it. Or they might go in the exact opposite direction and start looking for someone else to blame. Deciding that "fate" or "karma" is the cause, or "That's just what you get" or "What goes around comes around" is irrelevant and unhelpful.

If you are currently faced with devastating hurdles and difficult obstacles in your life, the situation is not necessarily a result of something you did or did not do. It might be that no one is at fault. Terrible things happen, but your faith will help you overcome and endure.

Whether you are a believer or a nonbeliever, it's impossible to separate faith from life, because every choice we make comes from faith in something or someone. For Christians, our faith is in Jesus Christ. The Bible says, "I am crucified with Christ: nevertheless I live; yet not I, but Christ liveth in me: and the life which I now live in the flesh I live by the faith of the Son of God, who loved me, and gave himself for me" (Galatians 2:20 KJV; cf. Hebrews 10:38).

This Scripture is saying that "living by faith" is our responsibility (Hebrews 11). Living by faith does not mean "blindly" believing in God, but "wisely" trusting him to supply our every need. Faith is believing that God has promised us a better world; and by faith, we have chosen to hold God to that promise and to take hold of that promise for ourselves.

The book of Job illustrates the life of someone living by faith despite terrible circumstances. Although Job suffered traumatic losses, he didn't lose confidence in the future. He really did not understand why he was afflicted; after all, he had lived a moral life and was an upstanding member of his community. But he never stopped believing that God would vindicate him despite his friends' assurances to the contrary. In the midst of his greatest suffering, Job still said, "I know that my Redeemer lives" (Job 19:25). This needs to be the battle cry of every believer in Christ. God is constantly asking us, "Will you live by faith, or will you crumble when you don't see or understand what I am doing?"

God's answer to Job was simply "I am with you." We might not understand why we are suffering or perhaps we think that we are being treated unjustly; even so, we have available to us a living God who loves us and strives to help us run the race set before us and fight the good fight (see 1 Timothy 6:12). I can recall a time when I was going through a "Job season." This was a period of my life that took me by surprise and challenged every ounce of faith and trust I had. I could handle the hurdles and obstacles when they were coming from the outside, but being attacked from the inside literally brought me to my knees. This testimony is regarding my children. After going through a painful divorce, there were unresolved issues regarding my children and visitation with my children. Out of nowhere there appeared an onslaught of accusations that challenged my character and ability to parent. I was devastated by the false accusations, because the lies hurt but also because of what seemed like the court system's bias. Even though there was no truth or proof of the accusations, I was denied custody. Many of my so-called friends turned their backs on me. I felt like I was all alone, with no one to believe me.

The situation got so bad that I was forced to endure ten months without seeing or speaking to my children. I fell into depression as my attempts failed to keep the faith and stay positive. It seemed every effort to seek justice and regain custody was denied, blocked, or postponed. I began to challenge God and ask him why this was happening to me. When I asked my pastor, he reminded me that everyone goes through a Job season.

At that moment I realized that in order to truly have a testimony, you truly have to pass a test. My test was letting go of what I could not control and reminding myself that in all things God works for the good of those who love him, who have been called according to his purpose. I then released my fears to the Lord.

As time passed, I realized that God's plan was not my plan. It took nearly a year for God to do what he needed to do in my life and my children's lives. I am proud to say that the seeds of love I planted in my children were not in vain. Despite all the wrong that was done to me, I still stand in victory. My children love me, and nothing and no one can take that away. I truly understand what Paul meant when he said, "Faith is the substance of things hoped for, the evidence of things not seen" (Hebrews 11:1 KJV)

In his classic book *Combat Faith* (Bantam, 1986), Hal Lindsey describes a few of the scriptural promises that come to us through faith:

> We are born into eternal life through faith; we are declared righteous before God by faith; we are forgiven by faith; we are healed by faith; we understand the mysteries of creation by faith; we learn God's Word by faith; by

faith we understand things to come; we walk by faith and not by sight; we overcome the world by faith; we enter God's rest by faith; and we are controlled and empowered by the Holy Spirit by faith.

The issue of faith pervades every aspect of our relationship with God and our service for Him. Faith is the source of our strength, our provision, our courage, our guidance, and our victory over the world system, the flesh and the devil. Faith is the only thing that can sustain us in the trials and persecutions predicted for the last days. It is therefore imperative that we understand exactly what faith is, how we get it and how it grows. (21–22)

Faith allows us to "see" God. Faith is the telescope that scans the heavens for the majesty of God, and also the microscope that magnifies his hidden wonders. Faith is the codebreaker that allows us to interpret and understand the meaning of God's words. Faith is the only path that allows us not only to "see" God, but also to draw near to his presence and fellowship with him. Only as we walk by faith can God make the darkness light before us (Isaiah 42:16) and enable us to see his handiwork (Psalm 19:1-3). Therefore, faith is the only thing that will bring us into the intimacy with God that we yearn for and that he so desires for us (Hebrews 11:6). Only as we see God as he truly is, and see ourselves as we really are, will we ever become truly pleasing in his sight. In other words, no prayer, no tears, no fasting, or no amount of good works without faith will alone ever make us pleasing to God.

Faith Is the Victory That Overcomes

Faith is the key that opens the door to our spiritual victory and enables us to walk triumphantly with Jesus. Only true faith can overcome the problems and tormentors of this world. To "overcome" simply means to use the free gift of God's grace to live in union with God and in a right relationship with others. Overcoming means that, with God as our helper, we can fulfill God's commandments to love God with all our hearts, souls, minds, and strength; and love our neighbors as ourselves. Our faith helps us carry the standard of Christ and wear his protective armor (Colossians 3:5; Galatians 5:24; Ephesians 4:24; 6:10-18).

Such faith enables us to maintain a relationship with God and be our best selves even in times of suffering. Even though "the earth should change, though the mountains shake in the heart of the sea" (Psalm 46:2), we can know that we are being held by God. We are to put our complete faith in no one and nothing other than God (Psalm 146: 3-5).

The Shield of Faith

Every morning I prayerfully put on the "whole" armor of God (Ephesians 6:10-17). But over the last couple of years, I have come to especially appreciate the "shield of faith" (6:16) as one of the more important pieces of that armor. I know that all the pieces are essential, but I have found a special benefit in taking it up. This is the piece of armor that prevents the enemy's arrows from piercing my heart and life. If we love Jesus, if we want more of him, we will be attacked. The enemy's game plan is to do everything in his power to undermine our faith so that we drop our shields, leaving ourselves wide open for attack. Thus, when we lose or falter in our faith in God and his promises, we open ourselves to temptation and will experience the sharp thrust of the enemy's killing sword. While you may not believe in Satan, in my experience he is our archenemy, and we need to attend to our spiritual defenses or risk disaster.

When we learn to make faith choices and trust in God *no matter what is happening all around us*, we hold up that shield of faith and it protects our hearts. Faith choices give God the freedom to work in our lives. The wonderful thing about faith choices is that God, in his perfect timing and his perfect way, will eventually align our feelings with our actions.

What does faith do?

To this end we always pray for you, asking that our God will make you worthy of his call and will fulfill by his power every good resolve and work of faith, so that the name of our Lord Jesus may be glorified in you, and you in him, according to the grace of our God and the Lord Jesus Christ. (2 Thessalonians 1:11-12)

What exactly is this "work of faith"? The work of faith, I believe, is simply choosing, moment by moment, to believe upon, trust in, and walk in the promises of God.

A vital faith is made up of a series of moment-by-moment choices. Only by the work of faith can we fully embrace God's promises, even though we may never see them fulfilled in our lifetime.

I know this statement declares a difficult truth, but look at the lives of Abel, Enoch, Noah, Abraham, and Sarah. Hebrews 11:13 tells us that "all of these died in faith without having received the [God's] promises, but from a distance they saw and greeted them." In other words, they fully embraced God's promises through faith alone. Such belief is our work of faith.

One of the lessons that God is teaching me in my own life is that his promises are true, but they will be fulfilled in his time and in his way. *My work of faith is simply to believe and trust in his faithfulness to keep his word.* God is in charge of the means, the manner, and the way in which those promises will be answered, and I am learning to accept this fact by faith. I am learning how to hold the promises that God gave me on that Olympic mountaintop in my heart, just as Mary did in Luke 2:19: "Mary treasured all these words and pondered them in her heart." As I keep my eyes totally focused on the Lord, he will show me when I can bring out those promises and say, "The Lord said this would happen, and now it is happening." This focus is my work of faith.

Faith Shines Light into Your Darkness

Faith lightens our paths and leads us from the realm of the visible to the realm of the Spirit. **Hope** turns our attention forward to what we do not possess. And **love** centers our affection on God and other people—love reminds us that our purpose is greater than ourselves and that preparing ourselves for the race requires aligning ourselves with God's will.

Broken and failed relationships often present seemingly insurmountable challenges and create daunting obstacles to overcome. A breakup is painful when amicable, and even harder when there is ill will. When you are betrayed, slandered, abused, or neglected, the situation can easily rattle your faith. I have discovered that putting my faith in people and materialistic things just does not work. Depending completely on income, social position, or even friends and family will lead to disappointment. Looking at things from only a human perspective instead of calling on God is a recipe for disaster. So, in order to prepare ourselves for success, we must truly apply our faith in God as part of our daily training routine.

There is nothing wrong with having friends, consultants, and counselors to talk to. It's smart and encouraging to seek wise counsel. But our faith comes from the Lord, and we should put nothing above that. God is the one and great "I AM." God will never leave you, and he will not forget about you. Whatever you are going through, however unfairly you have been treated, God cares, and your faith in God will see you through. Don't give up and don't give in to whatever you're going through. Trust in him, and he will bring you through.

Perseverance and faith during trials cause faith to grow. So be glad and look at your obstacles with a steady eye. When you continue to trust God in difficult times—enduring hardship and adversity—your faith puts down deep roots. All kinds of troubles may challenge your faith, but when you remain steadfast, there will be real and lasting spiritual growth. Faith that has endured suffering, failure, poverty, or ill health will not only be stronger, it will have been tested, refined, and proved. And it will be a ready help the next time trouble appears.

But I Can't!

Sometimes we can be so broken, so injured, that our faith seems to disappear. We might try and try to trust God and have faith, but it just doesn't seem to come. We simply cannot shake the spirit of fear that permeates our souls. Then what do we do? The Bible says faith comes by hearing "and hearing by the Word of God" (see Romans 10:17). "Hearing" implies that someone is speaking. And thus the Word has to be spoken and then it has to be heard, or received. To increase your faith, start by speaking it. And saying your prayers *out loud* is a good way to begin. Kneel next to your bed or with a close friend and pray out loud. Your prayers don't have to be fancy, but they do need to be from the heart. True, you can pray anywhere, but going into a house of God—a place of worship—and kneeling at the altar puts you in touch with the humility you may need to hear what God wants to say to you.

And if you don't already, hang out with other people who have faith, people who exude love and acceptance. Stop hanging around negative and stinky-thinking people. Be aware of and avoid pessimistic people who constantly talk negatively, These are the people who seem to always remind you of what you used to do wrong or what you are doing wrong, instead of what you have done and are doing right. When you are around people of faith who build you up, you will find that the dormant seeds of faith will again sprout. And be patient with yourself. Faith may not come to you overnight, but it will come if you nurture and tend it with Bible study, Christian fellowship, and worship.

For some people sacraments like Holy Communion are also important.

I knew a fellow once who lost his faith. So many bad things happened to him and his wife that it nearly broke his spirit. In addition, he had constant pain from an old injury. When I met him, he was almost worn out. But he was also a faithful member of his church. He attended faithfully despite his doubts and anger toward God. Actually, he really didn't say much to anyone about his faith except to a few close friends and me, his counselor. He continued to go to church and be around encouraging friends, and he continued to serve and volunteer for every project he could. He figured that maybe if he was around others who had faith, it would rub off on him. I didn't see him for years, and then one day I saw in the newspaper that he had died. While I don't usually do this, I went to his funeral. There I was blown away by the testimonies about his kindness, generosity, and service to the community. I'll never know what he ended up thinking about his faith, but his fruit was bountiful and sweet. I cannot help but believe that whatever struggles he had with God were somehow resolved. He finished the race strong. It really doesn't matter if you finish first, but what does matter is finishing well.

Faith is the reminder that your success is inevitable. Being delayed does not mean you are denied. At the appointed time, your purpose and goals will come to pass. All you have to do is keep the faith and know that God will finish the work that he has started in you.

FOCUS

I arrived at the World Championship in Spain in 1997 ranked number one in the world. I was feeling good, fast, and ready to go. I was in the zone! Everything was perfect. I had trained hard the past four years, sacrificing and totally committed to my goal, and there I was. The night before the heats began, I laid out my uniform, smelling the freshness of the U.S. equipment as I opened the bag. I went through my prerace routine, which included visualizing myself crossing the finish line in victory, and shortly afterward I said my prayers as I tucked myself into bed. Then I got *the* phone call telling me that my marriage was over. Are you kidding me? Right before the most important race of my life and you are calling me with this?! Wow. Needless to say, I spent the majority of the night arguing with my now ex-wife instead of getting a good night's sleep to be well rested for the next day—an unwanted and unexpected hurdle!

The next morning I woke up with bags under my eyes, feeling emotionally and mentally drained. I arrived at the warm-up track and realized I had forgotten my competition spikes (shoes)! I had to find transportation back to the hotel to get them and then rush back to the stadium. By this time, I had only thirty minutes to warm up for my race. Needless to say, when the race started, I was not focused, nor was I ready to compete. I took dead last, and my chances of becoming a world champion that year were over.

I remember sitting there after the race, a feeling of disgust in the pit of my stomach that I cannot adequately describe to this day. All the training, sacrifice, and dedication of a full four years had just crumbled right before me. It was at that moment I learned again the importance of staying focused. It was at that moment I made a commitment to myself that I would never again let anything distract me and get me off my game, prevent me from getting in and staying in the zone. Never! I may not win every race, and I may not be number one in everything that I do, but this is for sure, I will never defeat myself again.

Perhaps you, too, can recall a time when you self-destructed and felt the agony of defeat, not because of the challenge you were facing or the competition itself, but because of losing your focus, resulting in your defeating yourself. That is a painful and bitter pill to swallow, to know that the reason we did not succeed was because we kicked ourselves out of the zone by not staying focused.

People get distracted while driving and then accidents happen. If you get caught up in a good conversation while walking down a public sidewalk, you could wind up walking smack into a pole (I just did this. Jeez . . .). If you become wrapped up in the minutiae of living life—chores, petty frustrations, TV, fear, laziness, and self-doubt—achieving your dreams and goals will slip beyond your reach. You have to learn how to stay focused for success if you want to achieve it in any area of your life, personal or professional.

On Whom Do We Focus?

Seek ye first the kingdom of God, and his righteousness; and all these things shall be added unto you. (Matthew 6:33 KJV)

In our fast-paced world, it is easy to get caught up in the daily grind and lose sight of our true focus—God; but everybody's needs are different, and different people might focus on God in different ways. One person might memorize a Scripture verse each week, another might attend a prayer group or Bible study each morning, and yet another might have a goal of sharing the gospel message with at least one person every week. Any of these things can be effective in keeping Christ at the forefront of one's mind.

Not long ago, I went to visit an old college friend, who was a lifeguard at Manhattan Beach. We were getting reacquainted and had begun to talk about sports when, suddenly, I heard a woman screaming. My friend and I both looked toward the water and saw a male, around twenty-five years old, who appeared to be drowning. The man went under and resurfaced, coughing up water and frantically flailing his arms, trying to survive. I stood and started to step in the man's direction, disturbed and puzzled by my friend's inaction, but he put out his hand to stop me. As the seconds ticked by, the girlfriend continued to scream and the man continued to frantically call for help. Then, with no warning, my friend jumped up, dived into the water, and quickly pulled the man to safety. The man was okay and thankful that my friend had saved his life.

Later I said to my friend angrily, "Why did you hold me back? It looked like you were just going to sit there and let the man drown!" As I continued to vent, he abruptly interrupted me. And I will never forget what he told me:

"Mark, of course I saw the man in the water. I saw when he got in, I saw as he flailed around, and I saw when he began to drown. My teaching and experience have taught me that you *never* enter the water when the person you're trying to rescue is in a frantic state. This man was in his prime and looked to be about two hundred pounds. He was swinging wildly and out of control. If I had gone in and tried to rescue him at that moment, the only thing that would've happened would have been him knocking me upside my head, causing us both to drown. So I had to wait until he exhausted himself to grab him and pull him to safety."

Before any of us can be saved, we have to first stop fighting and accept help. As strange as it may sound, we have to surrender in order to be rescued. Likewise, God is waiting for us to surrender so he can pull us to safety.

A surrendered life is all about trust, trusting that God has your best interests at heart, that God can be believed and that he means what he says. Surrendering means trusting that all of your needs will be met and demonstrating that trust through your obedience. Surrendering one's whole life—needs, worries, pains, joys, and praises; the physical, the emotional, the mental, and the spiritual—takes the focus off one's self and places it upon Christ. Pastor Rick Warren of Saddleback Church in Lake Forest, California, put it something like this: "Surrender is not the best way to live; it is the only way to live. Nothing else works. All other approaches lead to frustration, disappointment and self-destruction." I personally can think of no better way to stay focused as a believer than to completely surrender my life to my Lord and Savior.

Once you have placed your life in the hand of the Lord, you are able to tap into the power and strength that lies within you. You will be able to do more than you thought possible, because you will be in alignment and in divine order. You will be able to do all things through Christ, who will strengthen you (see Philippians 4:13).

On What Do We Focus?

Finally, brethren, whatsoever things are true, whatsoever things are honest, whatsoever things are just, whatsoever things are pure, whatsoever things are lovely, whatsoever things are of good report; if there be any virtue, and if there be any praise, think on these things.
(Philippians 4:8 KJV)

When we prepare to face difficult challenges and obstacles in our lives, many of us focus on the wrong things. Most of us focus on what went wrong, where it hurts, who offended us, and how we feel. However, the Apostle Paul encourages us to meditate and focus on things that are pure and lovely and of a good report. In order to overcome our obstacles, knowing what to focus on is just as important as what not to focus on. Meaning, what we meditate on and give energy to becomes the center of our energy and attention. Instead of focusing on what has happened to us, it is more important to focus on what we can do to resolve or repair the damage resulting from what has happened to us.

Many of us need to heed the advice contained in the old saying "You can't cry over spilled milk." It is normal human behavior to cry over the situation and focus on the problem instead of the solution. Rather than becoming obsessed with the negativity and the outcome, however, successful people focus on what they can do to resolve the situation.

I remember a time when a friend and I were on our way to a sporting goods store to purchase some workout equipment. As we entered the crowded parking lot looking for a space, we noticed that one individual was just leaving. "Righteous," I remember my friend saying as he hit his hazard lights and waited for the guy to pull out. As the guy drove away and we proceeded to pull into the empty spot, out of nowhere a speeding Corvette dashed in front of us and took the parking space. Needless to say, my friend was angry and decided to have words with the guy. He got out of the car, walked up to the man in the Corvette, and spent five minutes yelling and giving him a piece of his mind. Meanwhile, I witnessed two other parking spaces become available that were closer to the store and that we could have easily pulled into during this five-minute verbal lashing that he gave the guy in the Corvette. Instead of staying focused on the mission at hand, which was to find a parking space, my friend became focused on the problem.

This simple illustration points to the importance of focusing on what you can do versus what has happened to you. Even though you may get knocked down, even though you may have a setback or a hardship, you can still recover and win much faster if you focus on what you can do instead of what has happened to you. It is hard, usually impossible, to control what other people do, but you can control how you respond to what other people do. Staying focused on your goals when you are confronted with an obstacle is crucial to your success.

When Do We Focus?

To every thing there is a season, and a time to every purpose under the heaven. (Ecclesiastes 3:1 KJV)

There is a season and a time and place for everything. Take time to work on your focus as well as time to rest. Knowing when to focus is just as important as knowing what to focus on. Focusing at the wrong time could be just as destructive as not focusing at all. For example, we prepare for winter by focusing on gathering wood for fireplaces; having shovels ready to remove snow from driveways; making sure we have a warm coat, gloves, and a hat; and adding antifreeze to the car. We know that the cold will bring issues that will easily turn into problems if we are not adequately prepared. The summer brings its own concerns as well. Our focus shifts from winter coats to swimsuits and beachwear and maybe new rigging for the sailboat. If we are not cognizant of the season, we won't focus on the right type of preparation.

Knowing when to focus and what to focus on is crucial to prepare for the race and hurdling over obstacles toward success. If you're going through a challenging time, focusing on the issues at hand is beneficial and necessary. Focus on those things you can do something about. You have only so much energy, so don't waste it by dwelling on and fretting about those things you can't do anything about. For example, if I twist my left ankle and go to the doctor and he examines my right ankle, he is focusing in on the wrong ankle. My right ankle might not be perfect, but he is not focusing on the situation at hand, and he doesn't do me any good either.

How Do We Focus?

How do we focus? Focus takes discipline and practice, and those things will be discussed later in the book. But focus also takes a willingness to prioritize by deciding what is most important. You have to decide what you want and if you really want to put in the effort it will take to get what you want. Then you have to lock on. If you have trouble doing these things, a coach or counselor might be helpful. Or it might be helpful to find someone who shares your goal.

I have a colleague, Zoe (not her real name), who, at middle age, wanted to get back in shape. She had run track in middle school, so she thought running would be her ticket to health. She knew what she needed to do, but too often she let other things interfere with going to the gym. She tried running on her own, but she couldn't stay focused on her goal. As it happened, she had a good friend who was a seasoned runner and agreed to run with her. It wasn't long before Zoe was running a mile—for the first time in her life. Interestingly, the friend's goal was not to run a mile, because she could do that easily; rather, the friend's aim was to help Zoe achieve her goal.

Forgiveness

Preparation for successful hurdling requires faith, focus, and forgiveness. Of the three, forgiveness is the most important and yet at the same time the most difficult. Forgiveness is a sensitive topic and something that many people discuss but few put into action. However, in order to truly overcome obstacles, forgiveness is mandatory. Learning to forgive is beneficial for our physical, mental, emotional, and spiritual health. Forgiveness helps to alleviate pain. It also helps you let go of the suffering that keeps you focused on your pain, rather than allowing you to be clearheaded enough to run your race and meet your challenges. Forgiveness is for the person being forgiven, yes, but it is also for you—for your own healing, health, and well-being.

We have all felt the sting, pain, and betrayal of being hurt emotionally by another person. Physical pain is the body's way of calling attention to an injury. It's your body saying, "Hey, pay attention to what is going on here!" Emotional pain, which is similar but more complicated because of how it is linked to your memory and thought processes, can easily result in bitterness and hard-heartedness. The suffering that ensues is caused by your thoughts, your *thinking*, about the situation. In the end, it is your thoughts that keep the hurt and anger alive, not the actual incident. Continued negative thinking can also illicit other destructive or wrathful feelings, and consequently, revengeful behavior. The bottom line: anger and resentment cause stress and delay healing.

I know firsthand the pain associated with forgiving someone—the laborious task of forgiving the unforgivable. Forgiving those who have betrayed you, deceived you, abandoned you, slandered you, or abused you is much easier said than done. However, it is imperative that we learn how to forgive in order to heal and move on to live in a healthy and functional manner. I am not minimizing the pain that you suffered, but merely offering you some insight that will assist you in overcoming the pain and help you move toward a more successful life.

Defining Forgiveness

According to *Merriam-Webster's*, *forgiveness* is the "act of giving up resentment of or claim to requital," as in forgiving an insult, "granting relief from payment," or forgiving a debt; or "to cease to feel resentment against an offender," as in pardoning an enemy. Forgiveness is a process of letting go of ill will, indignation, and/or anger against someone for an offense or mistake, and no longer demanding punishment or restitution. Said in a different way, forgiveness is giving up my right to hurt you for how you hurt me. It is impossible to live on this fallen planet without at some time being hurt, offended, misunderstood, lied to, or rejected. Learning how to respond properly is one of the basics of the Christian life.

When we forgive, we wipe the slate clean, pardon, and cancel a debt. When we wrong someone, we seek forgiveness in order for the relationship to be restored. It is important to remember that forgiveness is not necessarily granted because a person deserves to be forgiven. Instead, it is an act of love, mercy, and grace on the part of the injured person. And in the end, forgiveness often benefits the injured party more than the one seeking forgiveness.

The art of forgiveness is something that I have had to learn, and it has been a difficult lesson. I spent too many years holding on to bitterness, resentment, and hatred. I have spent endless days asking God to give me the strength to forgive, as well as the strength to forget. I have exhausted the Internet and the public library, as well as spiritual resources, in an attempt to forgive what I consider the unforgivable.

It's easy to advise another sister or brother in the faith that they need to forgive someone. It's easy to tell another person to "get over it" and "forgive and forget" when you are not the one who has been dealt the abusive hand and is faced with the challenging task of excusing someone's hurtful behavior. In my own trials and tribulations, I had to first understand what forgiveness is and is not before I could truly forgive.

What Forgiveness Is and Is Not

Forgiveness is not reconciliation. Forgiving someone does not mean you have to reunite or continue a relationship with that person. Many of us think that forgiving someone signifies an intent to continue the bad relationship, or stay in the abusive marriage, or remain in a dysfunctional environment. That is not the case. Forgiveness has nothing to do with reconciliation in terms of staying in an abusive, painful, or dysfunctional relationship.

Forgiveness is not condoning the action and behavior that took place. Again, far too many people mistake forgiveness for downplaying the severity of dysfunction. When you forgive someone, you are not saying the offense was "not that serious" or that "it will just go away on its own" without your making a change. Again, forgiveness does not diminish the seriousness of the offense or the pain you have suffered.

Forgiveness is differentiating the person from the pain. The reason many of us have a hard time forgiving is because we continue to associate the person who caused the pain with the pain itself. As a result, many of us suffer prolonged bitterness, resentment, and anger, especially if continued contact with the person is necessary for some reason. Remembering pain is inevitable, but suffering is an option. To begin the forgiveness process, we must separate the person from the pain. Once we do this, we can start the healing process. Instead of focusing on who did the hurting, we need to focus on what was hurt.

Forgiveness is not a confession. Forgiveness is not an admission of guilt or deferment of the abuser's accountability. Again, many people associate forgiveness with removing guilt. By forgiving someone, you are not saying that, once forgiven, they are innocent; nor are you saying that they need not suffer the consequences of their actions.

Forgiveness involves accountability. Identifying and acknowledging the accountability of the person who hurt you is an important step in being able to forgive. The abuser's realization and acknowledgment of his or her own accountability for hurtful actions against another is ideal and may be expected, but often does not come to pass. Forgiveness also begins with our being accountable by putting ourselves in a position where healing can take place and getting the treatment needed to regroup and move forward in life successfully.

Forgiveness is not amnesia. Many people say, "Forgive and forget," expecting us to spontaneously forget the offense that was done to us. Forgiveness is not going to magically make you forget the offense. For example, if a dog bites you, you can forgive the dog but still take steps to make sure he doesn't bite you again. You can remember and beware that this dog will bite you given the chance.

Forgiveness takes time. Forgiveness can take a long time, but it is worth both the time and the effort. A young girl was raped by her father. The sexual abuse began when she was about five years old. The mother never admitted to knowing anything, and the other siblings totally denied that such a thing could happen in their childhood home. But it did. The abuse went on for years. The rest of the family wondered why she was so different—why she was so wild, acting out every chance she got. When she became an adult, she checked herself into a mental institution because she was suicidal. She had suffered silently with depression for years, and actually the family was happy when she was diagnosed as bipolar, because at least then her behavior made sense. When she came to see me, she was addicted to prescription drugs and once again feeling suicidal. It took a very long time for her story to unfold. And then, during one session, she said in a hushed voice that her father had sexually abused her—for years. As her therapist a lot of things suddenly made sense to me, but she was still a mess and things didn't make sense to her. Over time, she shared her pain and showed me her emotional wounds. Slowly she began to heal. She had to work through layers of emotions including anger, rage, disappointment, bewilderment, fear, and rejection. It was only then that she was able to start talking about forgiveness—what it might mean for her, for her relationship with her father, and for her relationship with God.

I counseled this woman for years. She still takes medication for her bipolar disorder, and she still battles depression and suicidal ideation. She is choosing to walk the path of forgiveness, but it is a long and rocky road. Will she forgive?

Maybe, someday. Will she forget? No, never. But does she have hope? Yes, most days. And that possibility alone keeps her alive.

Forgiveness and Spirituality

Forgiveness plays a key role in our spiritual walk and our overall success. It also helps us to develop godly relationships. When we are injured, it is hard for us to be open enough to receive love, even God's. When people who say they love us hurt us, their actions confuse our understanding of what love is. This is especially true for children. Then when we say that God "loves" us, that just further complicates the matter. When we subconsciously associate love with being hurt, even God's love, we can find ourselves expecting God to hurt us too. At least for me, once I forgave, I was better able to open myself to growth and new possibilities in my life and in my relationship with God.

How to Forgive

First, make a choice. *Forgiveness is a choice.* Many people think of forgiveness as a process, and it is, but first the choice must be made to forgive. A choice is a conscious and deliberate action. Once you make the choice to forgive, then the process of healing can take place. Determine in your heart not to hold on to the resentment.

Second, give all your resentment—100 percent—to the Lord instead of trying to resolve it solely on your own. When we willingly take a stand before God of refusing to live a life without forgiveness and sincerely desiring to forgive everyone who has caused us pain, God will enable us to forgive, no matter how deficient we are in our strength. You have to make up your mind to release all of that hurt, pain, and bitterness.

Third, there is no shame in asking someone to help you. Runners have coaches for a reason. A lot of runners like to run on a team. Running with a teammate, especially one who can run faster, will help you run faster. Watching how a skillful teammate gets off the blocks can show you how to better start your race. Listening to the advice of a coach or counselor can help you trim seconds off your time by learning to move more efficiently. As you prepare to hurdle over obstacles, you want to take advantage of every piece of wisdom available. Forgiveness is hard enough; why not find ways and people to help?

Finally, do not be held back by your feelings. Forgiveness is an act of the will. Refusing to dwell on our negative feelings toward someone and instead looking for opportunities to bless that person, both in word and in deed, results in our betterment. When symptoms of unforgiveness well up inside us, instead of yielding to them, we must verbalize our will to forgive by speaking words in faith like: "I have forgiven that person by an act of my will. In the name of Jesus, I am not moved by what I hear or how I feel. I praise the Lord for God's grace that will help me forgive." By so doing, we allow the faith and the love of God to rule over our negative feelings. The good news is that with God, all things are possible.

When you think you can't move forward in forgiveness, find someone or something to cheer you on. For me, there is nothing like people cheering to motivate me and give me that extra boost to stay in the zone.

Forgiving Yourself

The forgiving that we've discussed so far has been directed at others. But sometimes we also have to forgive ourselves if we wish to experience more peace and contentment in life. Most if not all of us have been programmed from an early age to be self-critical and to believe that we are not quite good enough. Our upbringings can cause us to hold judgment, anger, and resentment toward ourselves, which pollutes our inner being and is a major drain on the energy we should be giving to preparing to race. Not carrying the burden of guilt, remorse, and regret will lighten your load and is key to helping you forgive yourself. Yes, you made some mistakes. Maybe you were fooled, and perhaps you hurt yourself and others in the process. But look to the finish line and concentrate on what's ahead and not what you've left behind.

Regardless of what we have done, we have a merciful God who will forgive us if we ask. Likewise, God expects us to receive forgiveness by forgiving ourselves. In my own life, I've had to forgive myself. Being raised in an emotionally and physically abusive environment, I've encountered a lot of confidence and self-esteem hurdles. I did not believe in myself and continually sought recognition and approval. I strove to please people and went out of my way to make sure everyone liked me; however, that behavior backfired and eventually put me under the hold of codependency.

According to therapist Jef Gazley, codependency is a relationship in which one person focuses so much on another person's needs and problems that the person forgets to take care of her or his own well-being and emotional health. The inability to say no when warranted and often putting the thoughts, feelings, and needs of others before your own are red flags of codependency. I made unwise choices and decisions that hindered my professional and athletic career. Looking back, I have many regrets. I've continued to struggle with forgiving myself for making ill-advised decisions, but with the grace of God I will find a way.

Several years ago I was on a bus at rush hour. I remember that I had just bought and was wearing a new pair of Air Jordan white tennis shoes. There was a tiny, innocent-looking woman standing next to me. When the bus stopped, the driver asked everyone to step back toward the rear of the bus. Everybody quickly moved back, except me. The woman stepped directly on my brand-new white tennis shoes. "Ouch!" I yelled. She had left a permanent black high-heel mark on my shoe. It stuck out like a sore thumb and I was initially angry. After several moments of her sincere apology, I said "no worries" and let it go. But the lady continued to apologize the remaining time we were on the bus. She even offered to pay for a brand-new pair of shoes. Again, I stated that it was no big deal and that accidents happen. But she still apologized and apologized and apologized! I had already forgiven her, so there was no need for her to continue to beat herself up about it. If we have made mistakes in our lives— and we all have—and have stood truly accountable for the mistakes and asked forgiveness, we should let them go.

Many of us are programmed from an early age to be self-critical. Our families, teachers, coaches, and society project their own judgments and insecurities onto us, as others have done to them. That's just the way people are and how the world works. But children lack the capacity to discern this truth, and they simply absorb what they are told. If you tell a child that he is bad or stupid, he will believe you. At some level he thinks, *Hey, this person loves me, so what they say about me must be true.* And if a child is continually told that she is bad, she will grow up to fulfill the prophecy made about her. This is not to say, however, that children do not need to hear when they behave badly or make dangerous mistakes. But if that is all they hear or even the majority of what they hear from you, it will be difficult for them to see themselves as people worthy of success.

When you clearly understand the roots and causes of negative self-judgment, forgiving yourself becomes easier. After years of criticism as a child, I grew up to be very hard on myself. We do not realize as children that the adults around us have their own issues. A child's interpretation of criticism is that there is something wrong with "me." The day I saw through this and "proclaimed myself innocent of all charges" was the beginning of my success.

But here is a word about parents. Now that I am a parent myself, I have a fuller understanding. One of the most difficult things for many people is to forgive their parents. This is the case for many of the men I see in my practice. No parent will meet a child's needs perfectly. One of my clients had a particularly difficult relationship with his dad. The father was well-meaning, but he just had no appreciation for the goals and dreams of his son. His father thought, *Why should I help my son? No one helped me, and I turned out stronger for it. He'll never go pro anyway.* On the other hand, the son thought, *Why won't Dad help get me to basketball practice? He always puts it off on Mom, and she can't get me there half the time. He has time to stop by the bar and have a few drinks with his buddies, though. Doesn't he care about me?* The son did turn out to be a pro, but he hasn't talked to his dad in years. And for years the son did one self-defeating thing after another, sabotaging his own efforts. It wasn't until he forgave his father that the son's game really took off. The son finally realized that his father had done the best he could. It may not have been enough, but the past did not have to shape the future. And the son really wanted his own kids to know their grandfather. There is a lot more to the story, but the fact remains that when the son forgave his father for not being the father he needed and wanted, the son's own self-defeating behavior stopped and he was prepared for new possibilities on the road ahead.

PASSION

Unleash the power of passion in your spirit. We hear the word *passion* used in various ways and in numerous scenarios. To understand true passion, one must truly tap into their purpose and be prepared with faith, focus, and forgiveness. If purpose is the engine that drives you to your destination, and preparation means that you have loaded up your equipment, then passion is the fuel that you'll use to ignite your race.

KNOWING WHY

We generate passion when we can answer the question Why am I doing what I'm doing? It was an Olympic year and I was standing near the practice track in my workout gear. The sun was beating down on my face, and my feet were being burned by the heat kicking up from the track. The temperature read 110 degrees in the shade, and yet here I stood in the middle of the practice field. To make things more interesting, I remember receiving a call from a friend inviting me to a pool party. He said, "There's going be a lot of family and friends there, along with plenty of food and festivities."

I had a choice between going to a party, swimming in a pool with 80-degree water, and eating barbecue with beautiful women and listening to music; and running myself to exhaustion in 110-degree weather. I tell you what, at that moment I had to ask myself *Why? Why am I out here putting myself through excruciating pain when I could be enjoying myself with friends and family?* I had to remind myself that I was there on the track because I was training for the Olympics and I wanted to win an Olympic medal. As I repeated that to myself, I began feeling the power of passion flow through my body. The sun wasn't so hot that it couldn't energize me. It was a clear beautiful day, and I was now, more than ever, ready to run. I knew why I was there, and the importance of my practice sparked my passion.

To be number one, you have to keep your priorities straight, and you have to remind yourself why your race matters so much. Discipline, dedication, determination, and, most of all, a passionate *you* are required to succeed in life. You can be as prepared as can be, but if you don't maintain your passion, you won't have that sense of resiliency you need to succeed.

STAYING MOTIVATED

After my workout on the track that day, I felt a sense of accomplishment and victory. I recall some bystanders who were watching me train in the heat. One commented, "You must be training for the Olympics." I replied, "Yes, I am." My purpose was obvious from my actions. My actions reflected my purpose and preparation, and my primary purpose during that season of my life was to represent the United States of America in the Summer Olympic Games. But I needed to stay motivated.

After representing my country in the Olympics and having won an Olympic medal, I remember coming home and having the biggest pool party ever. It was at that time when I realized I hadn't sacrificed going to a barbecue; rather, I had invested that day on the track in my purpose, which was to make it to the Olympics and win an Olympic medal. I understood exactly why I had declined the invitation to the pool party and worked out instead. Knowing why gives us the motivation, energy, and power to do what our purposes dictate. Knowing why fueled my resolve to face and conquer those obstacles that threatened my running the race.

Passion does not necessarily make you feel good in the short term—it was still 110 degrees that day. Rather, passion gives you the power and energy to do what makes you feel good for the duration!

PERMISSION

Many people seek approval from friends, family, industry leaders, and colleagues before pushing the Go button. They feel they should not move forward unless they first have everyone's approval or permission. Sadly enough, the most important permission to seek is often the last one sought by most people—permission from themselves. We fail to give ourselves permission to accomplish our goals and then wonder why we constantly come up short or rarely see things through to the end. If you do not give yourself permission to start, then you never will.

Picture yourself preparing to run a race. The official yells, "Runners, take your marks!" Everyone gets into the starting blocks, including you. Then the official says, "Set!" Everyone rises, prepared to go. *Bang!* The gun goes off, and everyone begins running *but you*. Needless to say, you will not do well in the race. Not consciously giving yourself permission is the same as not responding to the signal to go during a race. You will just be left there in the starting blocks.

Some feel that they do not deserve success. They have been brainwashed into believing they are not special enough or smart enough or rich enough or skilled enough to succeed.

They feel that they are not worthy of having a good life or living the life they truly want. Wow! I tell you, this is the biggest lie you can ever tell yourself. You do deserve to succeed. You deserve to run the best race you can and hurdle those obstacles. But my telling you won't make it happen; you have to believe it for yourself. Giving yourself permission is a good way to begin.

PERMISSION TO TRY

First, give yourself permission to try. *Don't beat yourself up!* That was something I said to myself before every competition. Many of us are afraid to try because we are afraid to fail. Allowing yourself the opportunity and giving yourself permission to try is a key factor in reaching your goals. Do not allow your fears to prevent you from trying. In order to do anything, you must give yourself permission.

I attended Mount San Antonio College and went on from there to receive a full scholarship to the University of Southern California. I couldn't believe that I would ever attend such a prestigious university. But one of the prerequisites of the scholarship was passing core classes with a certain GPA, and I had already failed several classes and was getting a D in others. I thought to myself, *How can I possibly make it at a university when I can't even pass classes at a junior college?* I even wrote the coach a letter declining the scholarship. I did not believe in myself enough to think that I could graduate from a university. I'd made too many mistakes in school, and my self-doubt was too great.

When I delivered the letter to the head coach, he said that day would always stay in my mind. After he read the letter, he said, "Mark! It's okay to lose, but it's not okay to beat yourself. And by not at least trying, you are beating yourself!"

I remembered hearing this story: Once upon a time there was a farmer who had an old mule. The mule fell into a deep, dry well and began to cry loudly. Hearing his mule cry, the farmer came over and assessed the situation. The well was deep and the mule was heavy. He knew it would be difficult, if not impossible, to lift the animal out. Because the mule was old and the well was dry, the farmer decided to bury the animal in the well. In this way he could solve two problems: put the old mule out of his misery and have his well filled with dirt.

He called upon his neighbors to help him, and they agreed. They soon went to work filling the well. Shovelful after shovelful of dirt began to fall on the mule's back. The mule became hysterical but then suddenly calmed down. From that point on, each time the men would throw shovelfuls of dirt on his back, he would shake the dirt off and step up. Finally, exhausted and dirty, but quite alive, the mule stepped out of the well and walked through the crowd.

The mule's actions showed a great attitude, a great way to approach life: shake it off and step up. Too often we hold on to what has happened to us for a week, months, even years. We cannot shake the experiences loose from our memories. Hanging on to the bad eats away at us and steals our joy, happiness, and peace of mind. Past hurts can create feelings of bitterness, resentment, anger, and thoughts of revenge. But we have a choice!

Just like that mule, all I had to do was shake it off and give myself permission to try. And even if I failed, I would shake it off and try again . . . and again . . . and, if need be, again! It took a lot of work, but I did get that scholarship to USC.

PERMISSION TO FAIL

Second, give yourself permission to fail. Many people deny themselves the opportunity to succeed because they are afraid to fail. In order to succeed, you have to learn how to handle defeat. Having permission to fail builds character strength and endurance. Do not be afraid to try, and do not be afraid to fail. No one is perfect, and even the greatest athletes, businessmen, and countless other successful people have all had to deal with failure in one way or another. Giving yourself permission to fail relieves you of the unrealistic pressure, expectations, and stress associated with trying to be perfect. Even the best baseball players usually don't bat over .500. That means they strike out half the time. Being perfect does not mean never making a mistake, but it does mean "complete." And a complete athlete knows his limits, his strongest competitors, and that nobody comes in first all the time. In fact, in order to achieve perfection, one must fail in order to learn from mistakes. Giving yourself permission to fail will actually allow you greater opportunities to succeed.

PERMISSION TO SUCCEED

Third, give yourself permission to succeed. When I tell my clients that they have a success phobia, they give me confused looks. Some of us can handle losing easier than we can handle winning. Allowing yourself the opportunity to succeed is easier said than done. Throughout our entire lives, many of us have been reprimanded, chastised, and conditioned to be careful, realistic, and adverse to risk. Oftentimes, our dreams are discouraged by others who have lost their desire to succeed or who simple don't want you to do better than they did. Consequently, when we put our minds to something and say we want to accomplish a goal, fear of succeeding is often present in our thinking. In order to truly succeed, we have to give ourselves permission to win. We have to give ourselves permission to succeed. In fact, we have to love, respect, and encourage ourselves on a daily basis, which will strengthen the process of allowing ourselves the opportunity to succeed. When we practice allowing ourselves and giving ourselves permission to succeed, we are one step closer to truly understanding what success is. Give yourself permission to be happy and follow your goals to a successful lifestyle. You deserve it!

Having an athletic background, I'd always prided myself on never giving up and never quitting. To my dismay, I found myself going through a very painful divorce. I was devastated and felt like a failure. I felt that I had not done what I'd committed myself to do. For several years, I beat myself up. I acknowledged and understood my part and realized that it takes two people to make a relationship work, but I still placed all the blame and responsibility on myself. This self-condemnation led to bouts of depression and self-destructive bitterness. It was only after I received counseling that I realized I had to forgive myself and give myself permission to be happy again.

When I did start to meet other women, my first inclination was still to deny myself the opportunity to get to know them. So I didn't ask anyone out for a date. If I couldn't succeed in my previous relationship, what would make me think I could succeed in a new relationship? I felt that I did not deserve to have a good relationship because I'd failed in my marriage. It wasn't until I received sound Christian counseling that I realized I could forgive myself and I deserved a second chance. When I realized that I had the power to give myself permission to be happy again, my life was given back to me. It was at that moment I started to enjoy myself, began dating again, and started to establish happy *and* healthy friendships.

I now understand what it means when we say that in order to have friends, we must first be friendly. We all make mistakes, and we all have things in our pasts that we wish we could change, but we must also learn and practice the ability to forgive ourselves and give ourselves permission to recover from mistakes and to be happy. Many people waste years of their lives punishing themselves for something that other people are ready to forgive them for. Don't waste any more time playing judge and jury. Forgive yourself and give yourself permission to be happy, try again, and, most of all, look in the mirror and love the person you see.

There is no formula for handling failure. You just understand that it is a part of life, and a bigger part of success. I always go into a race understanding that, yes, I might lose, but I also might win. Before every race, before every business meeting, I say to myself: *If someone has to win, why not me?*

On the flip side, however, there are *benefits* to losing and the rejection that often accompanies it. Failure is one of the fuels you can use to accomplish what you want. One of my clients told me this story: When he was in fifth grade, his class took an important achievement test. The entire class did well and the teacher wanted to show off how smart her class was, so she wrote all the scores on the board. The teacher mistakenly thought that by not putting the students' names with the scores, the individual student scores would remain confidential. She underestimated her class, though, because as soon as the bell rang for the students to go to lunch, they huddled and quickly figured out who had scored what. My client was horrified, because his score was at the bottom—the very last one. Actually, he was mortified and felt terribly ashamed, because up to then he'd thought he was smart. When his classmates asked him which score was his, he lied and said, "It's in the middle." But he privately vowed to himself that though he might be on the bottom then, he didn't have to finish that way. At that point he promised himself that by graduation, he'd be on top. And that's where he scored when he graduated—at the top of his class. He used what he saw as failure to fuel his future success. In fact, he said later that if he hadn't had that poor showing, he might not have cared so much about succeeding.

PERMISSION AFFIRMATION

When I was competing as a world-class athlete, before every competition I spoke this positive permission-granting affirmation: "Today, I give myself permission to succeed. I give myself permission to try, and I even give myself permission to fail. No matter what, I will not beat myself up. Because I am a winner, I am a champion, and I am an overcomer. I give myself permission to go out there and do the very best I can, and succeed or fail, I will come out a winner."

HOW DO YOU GET OUT OF A RUT AND BACK INTO THE ZONE?

Sometimes passion falters and we get in a rut. We repeat the same old routine, and racing eventually becomes just another chore. To get out of a rut, you have to have a sense of humor. Before I won the silver medal, one of the factors that led to my having a double hernia was that I was in a rut. During my preliminary races I kept hitting the hurdles. I hit hurdle after hurdle before I decided to fix the problem. I grabbed my sports drink and put on my flats, then went into the ice tub. Miraculously, the next time I went out to the starting blocks, I went over every hurdle with no problem.

Sometimes the way you get out of a rut is to stop struggling. Ruts can be like quicksand, meaning the more you fight, the faster you sink. I'm often invited to participate in golf tournaments. The courses contain water hazards, sand traps, and other obstacles. That is where I picked up a new nickname: "Mulligan." I started a recent round of golf with about thirty golf balls. At the first hole, I was determined to clear the water hazard. Fifteen balls later, I remembered my experience from running hurdles. I decided to stop trying. At this rate, I knew I'd run out of balls long before the end of the round. To get out of a rut, you simply stop what you're doing. You just have to give yourself permission to say, "Today just isn't a good day."

PRAYER

MY TURNING POINT

When I was eighteen years old, I was living life reck-
lessly in Los Angeles. I owned my own motorcycle and often
drove it at high speeds, weaving in and out of traffic. This
day was no exception. I didn't care. I didn't care that I was on
a suicidal journey. Behind my helmet, tears rolled down my
face, but no one knew. I was good at hiding my tears—good
at pretending that my pain didn't exist. I could hide from
everyone but myself. That is, everyone but God and myself.
But at this point in my life, I wasn't completely sure that He
cared either. He didn't seem to be around when I needed
Him. At least, that's the lie I chose to believe.

The dry Santa Ana winds chased me as I rode my bike
along Valley Boulevard. I could see the familiar railroad
tracks up ahead. They taunted me, called my name . . . dared
me to do the unthinkable. . . . The overwhelming desire to
die consumed me. I knew that my escape from this crazy
life would end my misery once and for all. As I came closer
and closer to the tracks, to my premeditated destiny, I felt

something tug at my heart. I knew that it was the hand of God. I tried to shake off the feeling, but the more I tried to deny His presence, the more I felt Him tugging at me.

I slowed my bike as I approached the tracks. The large metal crossing bar came down, bringing traffic to a standstill. My eyes throbbed and my throat ached as my salty tears continued to fall. Something made me look at the man in the van next to me. At first it didn't seem strange that he got out of his van and started to head for the tracks. I noticed that he was wearing blue jeans and boots. I became fixated, however, when I realized that he seemed to have a sense of purpose about him, that he was on a quest. He ducked underneath the bar and stepped between the thin rails of the track. He began to walk at a steady pace.

The high-pitched scream of the train horn brought me back to reality. I looked to my left, and about 100 meters down the tracks, I could see the train approaching. The vivid white smoke and the roaring sound of the engine didn't deter the man. He continued to walk toward the train, his stride determined. *Nah*, I thought, *he's not going to do it. . . . He's just waiting 'til the last minute . . . and then he'll jump off.*

The cars behind me began to honk their horns, and people started yelling at the man on the tracks, "Hey, buddy, look out!" They, too, were witnesses to this strange and surreal scene. In total horror and dismay, we watched as the train quickly approached him. The focused and fearless look in the man's eyes was heart-wrenching. He never once broke stride . . . never once showed any signs of regret or hesitation.

Wham! The train hit him, propelling his body at least fifty yards. It happened so quickly. I froze in disbelief. Somehow I was able to pull my bike to the side of the road. *Why did he do that? Why did he have to do that? What was so bad in his life?* I wondered.

The engineer and his crew jumped from the train and began to search for the man's body. I joined them, and it took at least fifteen minutes to locate the body, or what was left of it. I remember staring down at that body, feeling helpless and ill and angry . . . all at the same time. I didn't know this man . . . didn't know his name . . . but for some reason I felt a strong connection to him. *What was so bad that you had to go and do this?!* That's when I realized I could have been the one lying on the track. I could have easily made that same decision. God had stopped me, and at that moment He allowed me to see the consequences of this man's choice. He allowed me to see the hopelessness and despair it created.

At that moment I became "determined" to live. I knew that I wanted to live, to keep on living, no matter what. I realized that there was always a tomorrow, and that whatever awful things might happen, I would overcome them. I decided on that day that regardless of the obstacles that stood in my path and the hurdles I would need to "jump over," I would never again allow myself to become a victim. I decided on that day to be victor, not a victim. It was that day that I decided with God's help to be a champion!

The Bible states that "the prayer of the righteous person is powerful in what it can achieve" (James 5:16 CEB). This means that the prayers of righteous people are powerful and worthwhile. We all have offered prayers that we feel God has not answered or not answered in a way that satisfied us. But do not lose faith; God is not uncaring, and God wants only what is ultimately best for you.

God is love itself. But the converse is not true. Love is not God. How can this be? In the first place, our human thoughts and knowledge about love cannot begin to understand the kind of love God has for us. And second, God is more than love. God is so much more than any of our imaginings. So when we talk about the power of prayer, we are talking about being in relationship to the power that created the universe.

The power of prayer cannot be overestimated. The prayer of a person who is in a right relationship with God is powerful and effective. God listens to prayers, answers prayers, and moves in response to prayers. It has been said that "seven days without prayer makes one weak."

Medical studies have shown the power of prayer (for more information, see H. G. Koenig, "Research on Religion, Spirituality, and Mental Health," *Canadian Journal of Psychiatry* 54 [2009]: 283–91). Researchers studied two groups of people; one group was being prayed for and one group was not. There was a remarkable increase in the rate of recovery of those who were being prayed for, even though they were not told they were being prayed for.

The power of prayer does not flow from us; the power is not in using special words or saying them in a special way. It is not how often we pray or how long we pray. The power of prayer is not based on facing a certain direction or putting our bodies in a particular position. The power of prayer does not come from the use of artifacts or icons or candles or beads. These things might help you focus and concentrate on praying, but they don't have anything to do with how God will answer. The power of prayer comes to us from God, who hears our prayers and answers them for our benefit. Prayer places us in direct contact with the almighty God, and we should expect almighty results, no matter how God chooses to grant our petitions or deny our requests.

For example, if I am praying for a new relationship merely so I can flaunt my new girlfriend in front of my old girlfriend's face, then my motives are not pure. Likewise, if I am praying for money with the sole purpose of buying a fancy car to drive through the neighborhood and be noticed, again, my motives are not pure. When asking for something, it is important that we align our prayer requests with God's will as we understand it. I am not saying that a beautiful relationship is wrong or having a luxurious car is bad. What I am saying is that when we ask the Lord for something, we need to make sure our motives are genuine and unselfish. Because we are human, our motives will never be completely pure, and our prayers will often be selfish. That's okay. The important thing is to be in God's presence. If you spend time with God in prayer, talking to God and listening for God's voice for direction and comfort, eventually, it will show. How? In the fruit of your behavior. You will become more loving, kind, generous, and patient. You'll have more peace and be less boastful and arrogant. You'll have more self-control, and, I promise, your sense of humor will improve as well.

WHY IS PRAYER IMPORTANT?

I do a lot of praying, a lot of meditating, and make a lot of positive affirmations, because these practices keep me motivated. Many people say they are motivated. The question is: Are they "positively motivated"? There are two types of motivation. One empowers and the other disempowers, that is, it is destructive. Positive motivation results in joy, which is different from just feeling good. Joy is for the long haul; feeling good is only fleeting. Joy is a spiritual gift that comes from a relationship with God. For me, joy helps me look in the mirror and love who I see—a child of God. Try looking in the mirror and saying "I love you" five times. Try not to laugh or grimace. Do this every day for a week and see if it makes a difference in your motivation.

Too many of us are put down from birth. We've constantly heard: "No. . . . Stop. . . . Put that down. . . . Don't do that. . . ." When there is too much negative attention and too little positive affirmation, we stop hearing the positive at all, or we hear it only dimly.

How do you get to the point of loving the person you see in the mirror? Be true to yourself, tap into your purpose, tap into your spiritual beliefs, and do not give in to anger, frustration, jealousy, or irritation. This will allow you to really zone in on your race.

Besides putting you in contact with the power of all heaven and earth, prayer is important because it also connects you with love, mercy, and compassion.

When I first discovered I had a talent in track and field, I wanted to win. Like most people, I did not like losing or being teased when I did not come in first. I remember praying to God to win an upcoming race. It was a homecoming track meet, and everybody in the school and in the neighborhood was going to be there. I wanted so badly to win and place first. So I prayed and prayed, and I just knew I was going to win that race. However, when the race came, I finished in last place. At first I was truly upset and began to challenge and get angry at God. Then I heard a voice in my head say, *Why did you want to win anyway?* And then I heard another voice say, *What would you have done if you had won?* Honestly, if I had won, I would have pounded my chest and done an in-zone touchdown dance—pointed to the opposing athletes and said, "Ha, ha. I kicked your butts!" My motives were definitely not pure, and I needed a good dose of compassion. I did not want to win because I wanted to glorify God or to do my best and represent our team for the school. Rather, my motive was to hurt someone else or to humiliate them by rubbing my victory in their faces. Needless to say, I could have prayed until the cows came home and not won. But God did answer my prayer, because I learned a valuable lesson. I learned something about what succeeding really means and how much growing up I had yet to do.

God did not answer my prayer in the form I wanted, but God pointed me to the path that would help me succeed and overcome future hurdles. God saw what was at stake for the long run. I could see only what would immediately satisfy my wish to look good at the time.

SHARING FAITH STORIES

As you can tell by reading this book, my perspective and position on faith is that it is a relevant and necessary element to succeeding and overcoming obstacles and hurdles in our lives. Being a man of faith and a Christian, here is my faith story.

Several years ago, when I won a silver medal at the Atlanta Summer Olympic Games with a broken arm, the media wanted to know how I did it. I simply shared that "the Lord is my strength," and I gave all the honor to my Lord and Savior, Jesus Christ.

But it wasn't always that way. I've had my doubts and gone through spiritually dry times, but I continue to keep the faith. Coming from a physically and mentally abusive childhood, doubt and skepticism were easily at my disposal. It's easy to tell someone to keep the faith when everything is going well in your life. It is just as easy to praise God when things are going well in your life. However, it's when you're confronted with your darkest hour that your faith and how you show your faith really matter. A number of years ago, I traveled to Berlin, Germany, to participate in a track-and-field meet. I was quite irritated regarding everything about this trip. First of all, I was not guaranteed any money. In order to receive any compensation for running, I had to win the race, and even then the amount of money wouldn't cover my expenses. Considering I was ranked as the number one hurdler in the world, winning should have been no problem. Second, I had to sit in the back of the plane, which you might think should not have been so bad, except for the fact that I had to compete the very next day, and I'm more than six feet tall and have long legs. But to top it off, to my left was a woman with her baby, who likewise didn't like sitting still in the back of the plane. I may have felt like crying, but the baby did—every fifteen minutes. It was a long flight, and sharing my faith was not at the top of my list that day.

As it happened, on that twelve-hour flight to Germany there was another young lady sitting close by. I was reading my Bible, and I glanced up to notice her staring at me. With broken English she asked, "What is that you are reading?" I was not in a great mood, but seeing her genuine curiosity, I replied, "This is the Holy Bible," and I showed her Psalm 46:1-2: "God is our refuge and strength, an ever-present help in trouble. Therefore we will not fear, though the earth should change, though the mountains shake in the heart of the sea." Then I went back to reading, and we never spoke again during the flight.

The next day at the competition, I felt great and ready to run as I warmed up. *This will be an easy payday,* I thought to myself. I did my usual prayer before I got into the blocks, thanking God for giving me this talent, and then I waited for the signal to start. For whatever reason, on this day I did not react to the starter's gun. I was the last person to the first hurdle and the last person to cross the finish line. I was devastated and angry. I'd just lost $5,000 after traveling all the way from Los Angeles to Germany!

Before I was even able to gain my thoughts, a news reporter stuck his microphone in my face and asked me about my race. It was then the rubber met the road. I remember replying to the reporter that as long as I had another day to live, I also had another day to win. I said that a true winner does not always come in first. And that day I was still a winner because God is my refuge and my strength, even when I fall short of earthly victories. To my surprise, about two weeks later, I received a letter from the United States track and field headquarters. It seemed that someone had written a letter to me in their care, and they forwarded it to me. What I read when I opened the letter changed my life forever:

Dear Mr. Crear,

You probably don't know me or remember me, but I am the lady that sat next to you on your trip to Berlin, Germany. Please don't take this the wrong way, but I want to thank you for losing your race. Please allow me the opportunity to explain.

I was traveling to Berlin, Germany, to visit my mother, who was critically ill. She is what we call a "madame" and has a multimillion-dollar estate. However, I did not get along with my mother, and in fact we had not spoken in over five years. To be honest with you, the purpose of my traveling to see my mother was not to visit her, but in fact, to kill her! You see, I was in financial trouble and as the only heir, my mother's multimillion-dollar estate would go to me.

I recall her lying in the bed hooked up to medical machines, and I was going to suffocate her with a pillow. As I picked up the pillow and approached her, I did not want her to make any noticeable screams or noise. So, I turned on the television and turned up the volume so no one could hear if she started to scream. As I started to press the pillow to her face, your face appeared on the television. It was your competition that you were competing in. For that moment I paused as you prepared to run. Wow, I thought, I know him; he sat next to me on the plane. With the pillow in my right hand, I saw you run and take last place. Seeing the hurt and disappointment on your face sent a chill through my body. Because I also know about being disappointed and being hurt. But then when the reporter asked you about the race, what you said forever changed my life. I remember you saying that regardless of what place you took, you were still a winner. And how even though you were disappointed, you were confident in your faith and belief. It was at that moment that I looked at my mother and dropped the pillow as I burst out with tears. I thought to myself if this winner could lose a race and still say he's a champion, then whatever problems I'm having in my life and with my mother, I can win too. Thank you for showing me how to win even when I felt like I was losing.

And I'm happy to say that Mother and I have reconciled and we are learning how to be friends.

Wow! I thought. God took the little faith I had and used it in a big way for that young woman and prevented her from making a horrible mistake. But I learned something, too. Sharing my faith was simply planting seeds. God does the rest.

Noteworthy athletes such as Tim Tebow, Josh Hamilton, and Derek Fisher have publicly shared their Christian faith, but many people ask if professional athletes should use public platforms to talk about their personal beliefs. What about you? How would you feel talking about your faith in a professional setting?

There is a significant difference between giving a brief testimony and giving a sermon. If your faith is genuine, it should naturally show up in your conversations, even if you say something like, "Sorry, I'd love to come, but I have to be in church at that time." Or, "I had the best time at the church ball game last night." Or, "I heard this great story at church. . . ." Talking about your faith should be natural and not something you have to plan or sneak into a conversation.

Corporate sponsors pay athletes millions of dollars to wear and endorse their products. Athletes are given financial bonuses if they even verbally mention their sponsors, because companies know the value and influence of professional athletes. So it would only seem natural for a Christian athlete to mention his or her main sponsor, Jesus Christ.

I have a friend who used to work at a credit union. After having had accounts at several banks, she really appreciated the difference between banks and credit unions. She really loved working there. In fact, she believed in her credit union because she saw how much good it did in her community and for her friends. One day, as she was giving her pitch about the credit union to get someone to move his account, it suddenly occurred to her that if she could talk so freely about the benefits of credit union membership, maybe she could also talk more openly about her faith, which, all things considered, was much more important. She asked herself why was she so reticent about sharing her faith, when she could talk about the credit union at the drop of a hat. "No more," she resolved.

It is also true that sometimes actions speak louder than words. Some may feel uncomfortable hearing about God, and others may feel uncomfortable talking about God. If you are truly representing something, though, your actions should reflect what you believe. But also be aware that if you witness with only your actions, you are only pointing to yourself.

A friend of mine greatly admired a childhood friend of hers. As the years went by, she often thought, *Wow, he's a great guy. I wish I was more like him.* It wasn't until their twenty-five-year high school reunion that she learned the reason he was such a great guy: his faith. As they talked, she told him that she wished he had told her about his faith earlier, because it really would have helped her avoid some of the mistakes she made. He had witnessed with his actions, but she needed some interpretation. She needed a role model, but she also needed to know that she could have what he had.

MY STATEMENT OF FAITH

I believe that the Bible is inspired by God, who is our final authority on faith and life. I believe in one God, our Creator and Sustainer, who exists eternally in three persons: Father, Son, and Holy Spirit.

I believe that Jesus Christ, God's only begotten Son, died on the cross for our sins, rose on the third day, and ascended into heaven where He now intercedes for us.

I believe in the Holy Spirit, his present ministry, his indwelling, his baptism, his empowering, his importation of gifts for today, and his transforming power in the lives of all believers.

I believe that salvation comes by grace through faith in Jesus. Salvation is made effective in an individual's life by personal repentance and surrender. Upon surrender, we are regenerated by the Holy Spirit, enter a process of sanctification, and look forward to glorification.

This is what I believe. Over the years I've changed and clarified my beliefs and sought to practice what I preach. Perhaps it might be helpful for you to write down what you believe. Writing down and sharing what you believe, especially with a small group, can help you stay focused and accountable in your life.

PRACTICE

GOING FOR THE GOLD

As the famous saying goes, "Don't judge me unless you've walked a mile in my shoes." For me this means that giving advice is much easier than acting on advice. When I first heard about "overcoming hurdles," I thought, *Yeah, right, easy for you to say.* There are many people with good intentions who want to help, but who have not gone through the storm themselves. I believe that in order to effectively help someone get over obstacles, one must have gone through obstacles themselves first. How could I expect you to do something that I have not done or could not do if I were placed in your situation?

In my life I have walked the road of abuse, abandonment, rejection, and self-destruction. I have felt the guilt of my mistakes and pain caused by others' mistakes. But I have also helped a lot of people get in the zone. Success in overcoming hurdles is not easy; it can be done, but it takes practice.

BUILDING MUSCLE MEMORY

Practice makes perfect. In the athletic world, we diligently and consistently practice repetition in order to build muscle memory. Tricia Ellis-Christensen says that muscle memory is a type of movement that occurs so often our muscle-brain connections become routinized. Babies learn to walk and stroke victims learn to walk again only with practice and a lot of trial and error. The better the person gets at walking, the fewer falls; and finally, the person is able to incorporate walking into other movements such as running. Although the precise mechanisms of muscle memory are still being studied, it is known that as muscle memory forms, neural pathways are created and reinforced, so that the person doesn't have to think about the movement. Thus muscle memory enables movement to become an unconscious process.

When a person takes violin lessons, for example, the teacher and the student spend a lot of time working on scales and exercises. The goal of practicing exercises is to build muscle memory, so when a scale or a particular configuration appears in the performance piece, the student can play it with less effort. By not having to think about fingering, for instance, the student is free to concentrate on the other parts of making music, like dynamics or even following the conductor. The goal of building muscle memory is that the behavior becomes second nature.

A violin teacher I know told this story about himself. He was playing one of his first recitals in front of some famous judges, and for this competition he had to play from memory—no music book on a stand to prompt him. Naturally, he was nervous but also excited for the opportunity. He began. The first section came easily because he had practiced it the most, but when he came to the next section, he blanked out. He could not remember the next section. In his panic, he started the piece over again, hoping that when he came to that second section, he would remember. But he didn't. So again, he started over. He said that he must have started that piece over about ten times. Each time he repeated it, he played faster. Faster and faster he went. He wasn't thinking about what he was playing; he was just trying to remember the next part. Finally, in despair, he quit, expecting the judges to chastise him. But, to his astonishment, they applauded enthusiastically. They couldn't believe how fast he could play, and they awarded him the prize.

Using memory, muscles grow accustomed to certain types of movements. This process is extremely important in sports practice and training. The more often you do a certain activity, the more likely you are to do it as needed, when needed. If you've kicked thousands of field goals, exercise physiologists assume that the likelihood of being able to kick one during a football game is pretty good strictly because of muscle memory. You don't have to wonder, *How do I make this kick?* Your body already knows how to do it. It's a habit. You don't have to think about it, and you are free to concentrate on other aspects of the game.

We practice for success through repetition. We want to make success a habit, but repetition in failure also exists. To fully explore how to overcome the obstacles of life and succeed, we need to discuss retraining memory. A person who is routinely subjected to abuse, neglect, and disappointment throughout life can easily become accustomed to failing. Likewise, we can grow accustomed to being put down, chastised, and ridiculed, or putting down, chastising, and ridiculing others. Behaviors associated with abuse are repeated so often that the abused person often automatically "assumes the position," anticipating being hurt. If you find yourself continually coming up short or dealing with outrageous and difficult challenges, there is a strong possibility that there are some bad habits involved. It is imperative that you learn new ways. The good news is that you can build and rebuild your memory. But, just like learning to walk again, it will take time and a lot of effort, as well as support from people who care about you.

To start building muscle memory, you have to return to the basics. Like a music student playing scales and exercise, you need to start with the fundamentals. And in so doing, you will have to unlearn old habits. If you want to be better able to speak in front of other people, for example, take a class. If you want to stop self-defeating behaviors, seek out a therapist. But in every case, you will practice the fundamentals.

There is a saying that consistent practice is the mark of champions. Likewise, repetition produces consistency. In order to have successful consistency, you must have productive repetition. Whatever you repeat, you will master. Good habits as well as bad habits are learned and therefore become a pattern. I used to complain about repeating the fundamentals. I just wanted to run fast and not have to do the basic warm-up drills until I learned that it's the little things that make the big difference.

When I first began training for the Summer Olympic Games, I did not want to properly warm up. The average time for a professional athlete to warm up ranges anywhere from one and one-half to two hours! That's just warming up, then you go into your workout, which can take another three hours. Not to mention the cooldown after the workout. Before you know it, you're training eight hours per day, six days a week—which is the norm. Over time, I developed my basic training session. I started off with a mile jog, followed by forty-five minutes of various stretches, then another twenty minutes of plyometrics and technical drills. Finally, I ended my warm-up with a ten-minute sprint.

But one 100-degree day I decided that I would not do the tedious warm-up drills and instead jumped directly into my workout. On my first lap, I felt a light pinch in my left hamstring but kept going. It wasn't until my third lap that I felt an even deeper and sharper pinch shoot through my leg. Then all of a sudden—*pop*— my hamstring gave out, causing me to have to sit out for five weeks. Looking back, yes, an hour and a half to warm up in 100-degree weather is worth it. I would have rather spent an extra hour to warm up properly than spend the next five weeks paying the price for not doing so.

RETRAIN YOUR MIND

Part of retraining our minds is also retraining how we speak and being mindful of our choice of words. A common denominator of successful people is their positivity and speaking power. Likewise, a common thread among those who fail to reach their potential is the negativity, skepticism, and pessimism that come out of their mouths.

It is important that you speak life into your situation and not death (see Proverbs 18:21). Far too many of us speak negatively on a regular basis. Below are some common negative statements that we make, sometimes under our breath, but at the very least they loom in our minds subconsciously:

- I'm too big /too small.
- My job is terrible.
- I hate my life.
- My ex is evil.
- Nobody appreciates me.
- My boss is a pain in the (you know what).
- Only bad things happen to me.
- He or she is better than I am.
- I'm a loser.

In order to retrain your mind, you must replace the negative thinking with positive thinking.

Here is how I dealt with my negativity as an athlete. I wrote out on the left side of a piece of paper every negative possibility in my life. On the right, I wrote every positive outcome that contradicted the negative thoughts. I had more than fifty negative thoughts regarding myself coupled with at least forty obstacles preventing me from accomplishing my goal of making it to the Olympics and winning a medal. For example, on the left side I wrote, "I am too slow," and on the right side I responded with, "I will learn to run faster." Another negative thought was "Every time I've tried in the past, I've always failed." On the right-hand side I wrote, "I will learn from past mistakes, which will take me closer to success."

I spoke with a professional boxer awhile back. He was training for his fourth rematch against a heavyweight champion. I'll never forget what he told me. When I asked him, "How do you expect to win this fourth time, when you lost to the same guy the previous three times?" he simply replied, "I did not lose three previous times; I just did not duck."

Do not make the mistake of dwelling on your past defeats; instead, focus on your future opportunities. Success or failure is just one effort away. If you get up one more time than you're knocked down, then you will win. I always tell my students, "Try like you mean it . . . train like you want it . . . and prepare to accomplish it."

BE NERVOUS, BUT NEVER AFRAID

Keep in mind, there's nothing wrong with being nervous, but there is something wrong with being *afraid*. It seems to me that being afraid usually comes from not having put in enough practice. A lot of us succumb to the pressure when we're not confident that we have done everything we could have done to prepare. We panic and the pressure eventually becomes unbearable. Proper planning and practice prevent poor performance. When you practice, make it a habit to say to yourself, *Have I done everything I can?* And if you haven't, take steps to make a course correction.

BOUNCING BACK FROM DEFEAT

Overcoming defeat is one of the most challenging tasks we face in life. When you have done everything you could to succeed and still come up short, it's quite devastating. There is no magic pill you can take to make the pain go away. However, how you respond will determine how well you recover.

Several years ago I was ranked number one in the world in the 110-meter high hurdles. I had already captured some of the most important titles in my event, including the Grand Prix Champion titles, USA Champion title, and the Olympic silver medal. But one thing was missing: the World Champion title. Going into the World Championship race I had the fourth-fastest time ever at 12:98 seconds. I was feeling good. I was ready to go. The location was Seville, Spain, 1999. I had worked hard and practiced more than eight hours a day, six days a week. I was a drug-free, clean athlete. I had put in my time—blood and sweat day after day. I had done all the right things, and I was prepared for this moment. With ten thousand people in the stands, the quarterfinals of the 110-meter high hurdles were live on TV.

All cameras were on me as the announcer said, "Mark Crear is predicted to win." Standing behind the blocks, I could hardly be still; the adrenaline flowed from the top of my head to the bottom of my feet. My focus was like that of a leopard scoping out prey. My eyes were on the finish line, and I had to go over ten hurdles to get to it.

Camera bulbs flashed, daring me to blink. The starter stepped up to the line holding his silver-plated Magnum starter's pistol. "Corredores estan listos," he commanded. At that moment I got in the blocks. I could hardly wait. I was thinking, *This race is mine.* "Listos." . . . *Boom!* I heard the gun and let go. . . . *Bang, bang!* The starter pulled the trigger twice, indicating a false start. I walked back in dismay.

It was the best start I'd ever had. The official walked behind the blocks and pulled up the yellow flag signaling the false start. I was befuddled. I did not see who made the false start. The particular blocks we were using were known to be very sensitive and very inaccurate in detecting the false starts. No worries, I had one more chance. "Corredores estan listos," said the starter. I again got into the blocks, focused and ready. Sweat dripped from my hands onto the track. "Set." A runner to the left of me, a German athlete, flinched. *Bang! Bang!* Another false start. *That German caused the false start*, I said to myself. Once again I remember so vividly the official walking to lane 1 . . . lane 2 . . . lane 3 . . . lane 4. Next to me in lane 5 was the German athlete, but the official did not stop at lane 5. At lane 6, he pulled up a red flag. I had been disqualified. I could not believe it! I was in complete shock. The crowd whistled, which was a sign of disapproval.

The announcer spoke in Spanish, which I didn't understand, and then another official came to take away my blocks and remove them from the track. I was astounded. What happened? I had not made false starts according to the camera, and on the instant replay it was clear that the runner on my left had flinched, causing the false start trigger. But at that time I had to leave the track. My world was crushed—all that hard training, only to be disqualified.

As I walked down the tunnel, the cameras followed me, paying little attention to the race. I remember that a psychologist met me and asked, "Mark, would you like to talk about it?" It was such a devastating blow; NBC was covering this race. I do remember them asking me what I thought, how I felt, and whether or not I was going to protest. I heard them, but I was not listening to them. I was in such a daze as I sat there, hearing the gun going off once again . . . hearing the crowd cheer . . . and seeing someone else win "my race."

The pain, the embarrassment, the humiliation and defeat were hard to bear. This is the flip side of victory that comes with being an athlete, with being competitive, with having a desire and goal and falling short . . . the inevitable defeated feeling. I had a choice to make. I had one more race that season, the Grand Prix Finals, in Munich. I could quit the season and go home, or I could train and try to make it up in the next race. I decided to move on and go to Munich. But for the moment, I stayed in Spain and used the pain as fuel to help me prepare for the next race.

When those Grand Prix Finals arrived, I was focused and determined to take back what I had lost . . . *take it by force* . . . take it back by any means necessary. All I knew was that I was not leaving that stadium without a victory. The gun went off that day, and that was "all she wrote." I ran harder than I ever had and won that race, setting a new stadium record. I also regained my number one world ranking. From that experience, I realized that failing does not make you a failure. You are a failure only when you stop trying.

AVOIDING FALSE STARTS

INVESTMENT VERSUS SACRIFICE

Many of us feel that we have to sacrifice in order to be successful. While sacrifice is important, people recoil from the word's negative connotations. For me, the concept of "investment" works better because it is more positive. An investment is something that we give with the expectation of receiving a return. In the business world, it's called ROI—return on investment.

MOTIVES

Determining your motives is an integral part of success. Many of us do not succeed or overcome the obstacles in our lives merely because our motives do not reflect the success that we say we want to have. In order to succeed and become a champion, understanding the importance of positive motives versus negative motives is a must. Let's review the definition of what a motive is. According to *Merriam-Webster's*, a *motive* is "something (as a need or desire) that causes a person to act." If the "something" that your motives are based on is hurtful feelings such as revenge, remorse, or regret, you'll trip yourself up. These motives are unhealthy, and they'll lead you to expend unnecessary energy and wreck your "form." Negative motives are generally defensive in nature and will make you more vulnerable to anxiety and failure.

RED FLAGS

By common definition, a *red flag* is a warning signal. Warnings are crucial for avoiding potential danger. It is imperative that you establish a system to red-flag and mark as a danger anything that could derail your efforts to reach success. The people you spend your time with and the places where you spend your time can be red-flag areas. One summer I was fishing at a small lake. Every fish I caught was about the size of a dollar bill—too small to keep. So when I reeled in the baby fish, I took them off the hook and released them back into the water. My luck did not improve until it dawned on me that I needed to change my location. Those small fry were red flags telling me that I needed to relocate. I was doing the same thing repeatedly but expecting different results.

KNOWLEDGE IS POWER

Not true! *Applied* knowledge is power. Most of us have the knowledge of what to do, but following through and applying it is a totally different thing. When people apply the knowledge they have, then they become powerful. And knowing when to apply appropriate knowledge yields wisdom.

"YOU DIDN'T WIN A SILVER, YOU LOST THE GOLD"

Comments like these come from people who have never won a silver, bronze, or gold medal! Whenever you reach the top three in the world in anything, it is a major accomplishment and deserves to be celebrated. This extends to any task or goal you set out to achieve. Being on the "podium" is a success. The success is not necessarily in coming in first; rather, it's in the experience you gained pursuing your goal.

WALKING AWAY IS NOT THE SAME AS QUITTING

Letting go and walking away sometimes is the winning choice. Retreat is not necessarily a form of surrender. Rather, it may allow you time to regroup, reenergize, and restore, making you more effective when you return to competition in business or athletics.

Walking away from or letting go of something destructive or harmful is a positive act. Letting go of a toxic or dysfunctional relationship is a step in the right direction. Walking away from a dangerous environment is many times life-saving. Letting go of friends who mean you no good is considered a wise thing to do. It sometimes takes an incredible amount of strength to let go of a relationship, friendship, or job and just walk away. Make no mistake about it, though, one of the true character traits of a successful and strong person is their ability to walk away and let go when necessary.

119

THE TRACK RECORD DOES NOT TELL ALL

Some people wrongly say that a good indication of what a person will do in the future is what they have already done. It is important to understand the history of a person, but to judge people by their pasts is a big mistake. Just think about your life. Have you changed? Are you the same person you were years ago?

No one likes to have past wrongs thrown up in his or her face. When you repent and ask God for forgiveness, and when you truly make a commitment to change your ways, you can and will be a new creature. Old things pass away. Don't discount the power of change or the power of God by judging a person's future based on their past.

NEVER CHEAT TO WIN

Cheating is not trying. Cheating is exactly that, cheating. Don't believe that the only way you can be a world-class athlete or a professional in the business sector is by cheating, lying, or stealing. That is far from the truth. If you ask the most admired and successful people, they will tell you that hard work, discipline, dedication, and determination are how you become successful. Cheating is not a component of any formula for success! As mentioned earlier in this book, I was once offered illegal performance-enhancing drugs to help heal an injury. But it wasn't even a temptation. I didn't have to think about it for long. I don't cheat. I am a champion, and true champions don't cheat.

PRESSING TOWARD THE FINISH LINE

CONFIDENCE, COURAGE, AND RESILIENCY

As an Olympian, I trained long hours, maintained a positive attitude, and overcame my fears—all in an attempt to accomplish my goal, which was to win an Olympic medal. Although you may not be vying for any medals, you can learn about triumphing over the pressures and stresses of life. Here are some hurdles you need to check off your list as you race toward the finish line.

FEAR OF HAVING FUN

When you take the fun out of a game, it is no longer a game. In order to excel, keep the fun in whatever you are doing. When you remove the fun, typically it is replaced with stress. Rely on your courage, endurance, and sense of fair play as you meet your challenges and achieve success. You may not receive a gold medal, but you can succeed just the same.

BELIEVE IT

Give yourself something to believe in. The number one question I get about my Olympic victories is: "What goes through your mind just before you race?" My reply is simply: "I ask myself if I have done everything in my power to win this race. Answering yes builds my confidence." Believing in your work ethic and spending the time necessary to perfect your craft will magnify your chances of victory.

FEAR OF FAILURE

For some, failure results in humiliation and the loss of self-esteem. But when the goal is to perform to the best of your ability, you can feel good about yourself even when you don't take first place. The essential thing is not to have conquered but to have fought well. Stay focused on your growth and the steps you take, not the outcome.

FEAR OF SUCCESS

Does thinking about what might happen if you actually win stop you in your tracks and paralyze your continued progress? Do you fear losing the encouragement you received as the underdog if you win? Are you afraid that if you succeed once, you will be expected to succeed every time? If any of these fears are holding you back, you will benefit by addressing them, with the help of a friend or counselor, as soon as possible. Focus on the benefits of winning for yourself as well as others.

FEAR OF COMPETITION

Performance anxiety is a common and familiar phobia, and I'm no stranger to it. In fact, a little stage fright is actually a good thing, because it shows you care. And physiologically, it gets your heart pumping and your adrenaline flowing. But for some, anxiety and stage fright can be debilitating, so here are a few techniques you can employ to alleviate the symptoms:

1. Put the competition into perspective. No one is going to die if they win or don't win.

2. Breathe deeply, using your stomach muscles. When you are anxious, you have a tendency not to breathe. You hold your breath, preventing oxygen from getting to your muscles.

3. Concentrate on your own actions, not the actions of those around you.

4. Practice, practice, practice. Proper planning prevents poor performance!

FEAR OF RISK

In order to succeed as Olympians, athletes need to conquer their fear of the unknown and go for the gold anyway. According to Canadian hockey great Wayne Gretzky, "You miss 100 percent of the shots you never take." Don't be afraid to try or afraid to fail.

FEAR OF CHANGE

Regardless of what elements, circumstances, and schedules change, being able to adjust while you stay focused is the key. When creating your game plan of success, allow room and time for the unknown and spontaneous changes that may occur.

FEAR OF PAIN

No pain . . . no gain! You can't be afraid of working hard and doing what it takes to get what you want. Stay focused on the target instead of the steps to reach it. Take those steps one at a time. Keep in mind the determination you need to succeed as you struggle to prevail.

Remember, if someone has to win . . . why not *you*?!

WORDS OF ENCOURAGEMENT

Don't worry about your haters. Your haters can't do nothing with you. These lyrics from "God Favored Me," by Hezekiah Walker, have encouraged me during my darkest hours. I share them with you in the hope that they will encourage you as well. One thing I know is that there are times in all our lives when we feel all alone, when friends and family turn their backs on us. Likewise, there are times when we make bad choices and mistakes. But with the favor of God, we can still recover, fly over those hurdles, and finish the race.

EPILOGUE

Standing on the victory podium and receiving my second consecutive Olympic medal was overwhelming. Tears ran down my face as silence swept through the stadium and the national anthem played. It finally hit me. For the first time, I realized that although I had to overcome huge hurdles throughout my life, I could proudly say, "I am still here, and look at what I've accomplished!" In addition to my two Olympic medals, I am also an ordained minister, a PhD, a therapist, a businessperson, and an author. People might look at me and think that I am lucky, that I probably grew up on easy street. That is far from the truth. What I am, though, is blessed. My life has taught me to never judge a person if I haven't walked in their shoes and to never judge by appearances alone. Life has also taught me to look at success from the inside, not from the outside. I've realized that failing does not make you a failure, but not trying does.

I still have hurdles to overcome. I'm still running the race. As I reflect, I realize that the abusive treatment I received as a child conditioned me to be drawn to the same type of abusive treatment as an adult. As a result, I have at times attracted people who would abuse me rather than those who would care for me. Consequently, I ended up in abusive relationships again and again. I realize now that my biggest hurdles were insecurity and lack of confidence. I spent half of my life looking for someone to love me, instead of looking inside and loving myself. I know today that all I need to succeed in life is within me, and what I lack, God will provide. Because of this revelation, I have not allowed the negative people around me to affect me as much. Have they changed? Not really, but I have. I no longer carry the burdens of other people's problems. I now realize that I cannot control what other people do, but I can control how and if I allow their actions to affect me. I now can differentiate between others' problems and my problems; in the past I would at times take responsibility for everyone else's issues. If a store clerk was rude to me, it was somehow my fault. If a relationship ended, it was surely my fault. If I tripped and fell, I must have done something to deserve it. Well, not anymore. I continue to learn that sometimes bad things happen to good people, and it's no reflection on one's religion, personality, or skin color.

Life still is not easy. I've had to retrain and remind myself of who is in ultimate control—God Almighty. He is the great "I AM." Through him, I can do all things. Through him, I'm more than a conqueror. Finally, I realize that pain is inevitable, but suffering is an option. I choose not to suffer anymore.

I also realize that love and support come in many different forms. I have been blessed with many nurturing mothers and fathers during my journey. It didn't matter that they were not my biological parents. Likewise, instead of taking the view that my mother did not love me, I have chosen to look at it as if she were called to be a blessing to someone else in need. When I came to terms with the fact that my mom showed others the love and support she denied me, I realized her actions were not a direct reflection on my self-worth or even her love for me, but rather that the Lord was using her to bless someone as he blessed someone to help me. I was finally released from that burden of lies, but it took me a long time to accept this and heal. I was and still am all about family, but now I have a better understanding of its real meaning. Sometimes the Lord places other people in your life to give you what you need, and it's up to you to humble yourself enough to receive it.

THE LAST HURDLE

Even though the road is not always smooth, I now know how to deal with painful things in a healthy and productive manner. I am determined to keep running the race and stand on the victory podium— the victory podium of life. And most important, in spite of my past and because of my past, I can look in the mirror and love the person I see, the person God created me to be! I now have the confidence that no matter what, I am going to make it. If I fall down, I will get back up. If I'm disliked, I'll find new friends. If I sink, then I'll learn how to swim. If I fail, I will try again. No matter what, I will make it. I am not a victim anymore. I am a victor! And if I can make it, then you can make it, too. I'm here to coach you and cheer you along. Together we can break the tape. The race is not given to the swift, nor the battle to the strong, but to those who endure to the end.

ABOUT THE AUTHOR

Rev. Mark Crear, PhD, is not only an anointed man of God but also an ordained pastor, published author, Board Certified Professional Christian Counselor (BCPCC), Certified Life and Business Coach, and an Olympic champion. Mark is currently president of Mark Crear Ministries, President of the Multi-Cultural Christian Counselors (MCCC), Divisions of American Associations of Christian Counselors, AACC). Dr. Crear earned his BA in Sociology from the University of Southern California and his MA and PhD in Christian Counseling and Christian Theology from ITU.

Mark has traveled the world, preaching and presenting keynotes, seminars, and inspirational messages to churches and business organizations. Mark has a passion for emotional and mental healing, and he draws on his unique Olympic experience to motivate, counsel, and teach. Mark reminds us that hurdles are an inevitable part of life, but it is how we deal with them that determine our success. Dr. Crear's message is about conquering and getting over life's hurdles. Those who hear Mark speak leave with a new perspective on dealing with obstacles. People who hear him speak say that it is no surprise that Dr. Crear is considered a symbol of strength, integrity, hard work, and perseverance. Often referred to as "The Hurdler," Mark offers encouragement that is faith-sensitive, clinically sound, and easily applicable.

For more information, go to www.mc-ministries.com.

DISCARD

248.4 CREAR

Crear, Mark.
In the zone

METRO

R4001286683

METROPOLITAN
Atlanta-Fulton Public Library

CPSIA inf
Printed in t
LVOW06s

772023